BUDDHISM IN NORTH INDIA AND PAKISTAN

Bibliotheca Indo-Buddhica Series No. 191

BUDDHISM IN NORTH INDIA AND PAKISTAN

D. C. AHIR

Sri Satguru Publications
A Division of
Indian Books Centre
Delhi, India

Published by :
Sri Satguru Publications
A Division of
Indian Books Centre
Indological and Oriental Publishers
40/5, Shakti Nagar,
Delhi-110007
(India)

ISBN 81-87030-586-1

First Indian Edition : Delhi, 1998

Published by Sunil Gupta for Sri Satguru Publications a division of Indian Books Centre, 40/5, Shakti Nagar, Delhi-110 007, India and printed Mudran Bharti, Delhi+110 009

CONTENTS

Preface

This book presents a historical survey of Buddhism through the ages in the modern States of Punjab, Haryana, Delhi and Himachal Pradesh in India, and West Punjab, Sind and North West Frontier Province in Pakistan. In other words, it covers the area from Delhi to Peshawar.

Buddhism came to Punjab through the Buddha himself, and gained a good hold in the Punjab–Gandhara region within 300 years of the *Mahaparinirvana* of the Buddha. Thereafter, for more than 1,000 years, Buddhism was the predominent religion of the people of the region. During that period, a galaxy of Buddhist saints, scholars, artists, poets and philosophers like Nagasena, Asvaghosha, Asanga and Vasubandhu not only enriched the culture of the North–West region but also influenced and moulded the destinty of Buddhism as a whole. Three of the illustrious Buddhist kings of India: Milinda, Kanishka and Harsha flourished in the united Punjab, while the fourth, the most renowned Buddhist Emperor, Asoka, also started his career in the Punjab.

Later, under the weight of political and religious upheavels, Buddhism disappeared from the plains but it managed to survive in some hilly tracts, and is even today a living faith in the valleys of Lahul, Spiti and Kinnaur in Himachal Pradesh. Buddhism came to life in Delhi, the Capital of India, in 1939 with the establishment of the first Buddha Vihara by the Maha Bodhi Society of India. By now, Delhi has become a prominent centre of Buddhist culture and studies. The Buddhist revival movement is also making a slow and steady progress in Punjab, Chandigarh and Haryana. Even a modern Buddha Temple has come up in Pakistan also.

D.C. Ahir

Chapter–I

Buddha's Visit to Punjab

In the sixth century B.C. when the Buddha was born, Northern India was divided into many monarchical and non–monarchical States. The names of the monarchical States were Anga, Magadha, *Kāsi*, Kosala, Vajji, Malla, Chedi, Vatsa, *Kurū*, *Pānchala*, Matsya, Saursena, Asmaka, Avanti, *Gandhāra* and Kamboja. The non–monarchical States were those of the Sakyas of Kapilavastu, the Mallas of *Pāva* and Kushinara, the Lichhavis of *Vaisāli*, the Videhas of *Mithilā*, the Koliyās of Ramgama, the Bulis of Allakapa, the Kalingas of Resaputta, the Mauryas of Pipphalvana and the Bhaggas of Sumsumara Hill.

Gautama the Buddha was born in B.C. 563[1] at Lumbini, near Kapilavastu[2], the capital city of the Sakyas. He was the son of King Suddhodana and Queen *Mahāmāya*[3]. As a prince, he grew up in the midst of luxury, beauty and plenty. But slowly and slowly he was getting weary of his surroundings and was becoming more and more contemplative. By the time *Siddhārtha* was 29, his mental make–up had crystalysed. He was anxious to find a solution to the problem of Sufferring which had particularly pricked his conscience on seeing an old man, a sick man and a dead man in succession while he was on his way to the park. Then his only son, *Rāhula* was born. This provided him an occasion to take the fateful decision of leaving his palace–home, the life of luxury and pleasure, and to seek solution of his mental unrest in the homeless life of an ascetic.

After leaving Kapilavastu, the Prince turned mendicant trekked on foot and reached Rajagriha (Rajgir) which was then renowned as the abode of the great philosophers and leaders of thought. Not satisfied, with the teachings of Alāra Kalāma and Uddaka Rāmaputta, he marched torwards the forest of Urūvela, some 40 miles away.

The five *Parivrajakas* whom he had met at Rajagriha also joined him there. Together they started practising asceticism. For six years, the Bodhisattva practised rigid austerities and self–mortification. Still he could not attain what he sought. Convinced of the futility of mortificatin of the flesh, he abandoned the path of fasting, and accepted a bowl of rice pudding offered by Sujata, daughter of the Chief of the neighbouring village, Ṣenani. Annoyed with Gautama on partaking of food, his five companions left him. Thus the Buddha–to–be was left alone to pursue his path.

Having refreshed himself with food, the Bodhisattva reflected on his past experiences which had failed. Determined to achieve enlightenment; to know the ultimate truth, he came to the large *pipal* tree on the right bank of the river *Nerañjara*, now known as Bodh Gaya, seven miles from the present day city of Gaya in Bihar. There he sat crosslegged, determined not to leave that place until he had attained the supreme and absolute wisdom. On the fateful night when Gautama was about to attain the Buddhahood,the *Māra*, the Lord of evil thoughts and evil passions, swung into action and attempted in various ways to thwart his efforts. But all the efforts of *Māra* failed, and he disappeared discomforted. Then, on the dawn of the Full Moon day in the month of *Vaisākha*, Gautama atained omniscience, supreme enlightenmnt. Thus at the age of 35, he became the Buddha, the Enlightened One, the Awakened One. The Buddha is also known as the *Tathāgata*–the Perfect One; *Bhagava*–the Blessed One; *Sambuddha*–the Perfectly Enlightened One; Sakyamuni–the Sage of the Sakyas; and *Sugata*–the Happy One or the Accomplished One.

The Buddha, at last, rediscovered the way already traversed by the earlier Buddhas. He was tempted to keep the 'Knowledge to Himself', and *Brahmā* Sahampati had specifically to implore Him to disseminate the spiritual illumination for the benefit of the suffering humanity. Having enjoyed the bliss of *Nirvāṇa* for seven weeks, the Buddha got up, gazed with reverence at the Bodhi Tree, and thoughtfully proceeded to the deer park (Mrigadava) at Isipatana, modern Sarnath, near Varanasi in Uttar Pradesh.

On seeing Gautama coming towards them, the five ascetics, who had been ealier fellow—travellers at *Urūvela,* decided not to welcome him saying that 'by abandoning austerities and turning to a life of luxury, Gautama had committed a sin and was not worthy of respect'. But when the Buddha came near, all the five *Parivrajakas* involuntarily rose from their seats and greeted him. Impressed by his dignified manners and his personality, they treated him like a distinguished guest.

Unfolding the new path discovered by him, the Buddha said, "Two extremes there are, O monks, which he who strives after enlightenment must avoid, which two ? A life addicted to pleasure which is vulgar and worthless and a life given to self–mortification which is painful and equally profitless"[4]. Then the Buddha enunciated the Four Noble Truths: Suffering; its Causes; its Cessation; and the path leading to the Cessation of Suffering. And added that the way to *Nibbāna,*emancipation, or the path that leads to Cessation of Suffering, higher wisdom and peace of mind is the Noble Eightfold path. This path consists of : Right Understnding, Right Thought, Right Speech, Right Action, Right Livelihood, Right Effort, Right Mindfulness, Right Concentration.

Of the eight factors of this path, the first two are grouped under the heading of Wisdom, the following three under Morality, and the last three under Concentration. But according to the order of development the sequence is as follows : 1. Morality (*Sīla*), 2. Concentration (*Samādhi*), and 3. Wisdom (*Paññā*).

Morality (*Sīla*) means pure and honest living avoiding killing, stealing, lying, sexual misconduct and intoxicants.

Concentration (*Samādhi*) enables a devotee to overcome the five hindrances which come in the way of a person trying to practise the Noble Eightfold Path. These hindrances are : convetousness, ill–will, sloth and torpor, doubt and indecision. Wisdom (*Paññā*) means giving up of belief in the efficacy of rites and ceremonies; abandonment of superstition and supernaturalism; giving up of all doctrines which are mere speculations.

The first Sermon of the Buddha at Sarnath is known as the *'Dhammachakra Pravartana'*, the Turning of the Wheel of Law, and constituted the beginning of the Holy, Spiritual and Cultural Empire of Buddhism. Annata Kondana, Bhadiyya, Vappa, Mahanama and Assaji, popularly known in the Buddhist Texts as *Panchvaggiya Bhikkhūs*, were the first members of the *Saṅgha* established by the Master. The sixth person to join this Monastic Order was Yasa, who was the son of a rich merchant of Varanasi but he had no liking for all these luxuries. One day he was strolling on the banks of the river Varuna in somewhat dejected mood.. Lord Buddha, who was also there, heard him saying 'I am in trouble, I am in distress.' The Blessed One approached him, consoled him and delivered to him relevant discourse which removed Yasa's doubts and he became a *Bhikkhū*. Four friends of Yasa, namely, Vimala, Subahu, Puranajina and Gawampati, sons of the noble families of Varanasi also became Buddha's disciples. Then another fifty of their friends followed their example and joined the *Saṅgha*, making a total of sixty monks. Then the Buddha advised all His first sixty disciples to go and preach the Doctrine glorious. He said: "Go Ye, O *Bhikkhūs,* and wander forth for the gain of the many, for the welfare of the many, in compassion for the world, for the good, for the gain, for the welfare of the gods and men. Proclaim O *Bhikkhūs,* the Doctrine glarious, preach ye a life of holiness, perfect and pure."[5]

For the next forty-five years, the Blessed One travelled constantly from town to town, village to village, preaching His message of equality; of hope and peace; of kindness and compassion. As small rivulets flow towards the ocean so rushed the recluses, scholars, philosophers and lay folk towards the Buddha. The Buddha did not show any preference for any group or class of people. Irrespective of caste, colour and status, He admitted all into the *Saṅgha* who were willing to lead a holy life. His disciples, both monks and laity, therefore, came from all walks of life. They included rich and poor, high and holy, and low and lowly.

After having led for 45 years a very strenuous and selfless life in teaching the beauty of charity, the joy of renunciation, the need for simplicity and equality, the Great Buddha passed into *Mahāparinirvāna* at the age of eighty at Kushinara on the Full Moon day of *Vaisākha* in BC. 483 but left a great heritage for the humanity.

The teachings of the Buddha are preserved in the *Pāli Tipitaka* (Skr: *Tripitaka*). The three *Piṭakas* or 'Baskets of the law' are: the *Vinaya–Piṭaka,* the *Sutta–Piṭaka,* and the *Abhidhamma Piṭaka.* Of these,–the *Sutta–Piṭaka* consists chiefly of discourses delivered by the Buddha at various places during His *Cārikas* (preaching tours). The *Sutta–Piṭaka* is divided into five *Nikāyas,* groups or collections. The *Digha Nikāya* has 34 'long discourses' arranged in three *vaggas* or series. The *Majjhima Nikāya* is the collection of 'middle length sermons.' It has 152 *suttas* arranged in fifteen *vaggas.* The *Saṁyutta Nikāya* has in all 2841 *suttas* classed in 56 *Saṁyuttas.* The *Aṅguttara Nikāya* has 2308 *suttas* divided into 174 *vaggas.* The *Khuddaka Nikāya* contains fifteen independent books: *Khuddaka–Pātha, Dhammapada, Udāna, Itivuttaka, Sutta–Nipatā, Vimāna–Vatthu, Peta–Vatthu, Thera–gātha, Therī–gātha, Jātaka, Niddesa, Patisambhida, Apadana, Buddhavaṁsa,* and *Cariyā–Pitaka.*

Though the *Cārikas* of the Buddha were mainly confined to North-East India or say to Anga, Magadha, *Kāsi.* Kosala, Vajji, Malla, Chedi, Avanti, Kapilavastu, *Vaisāli;* and Pava–Kushinara States of those days but He occasionally travelled beyond these limits also. Here we will endeavour to trace the footsteps of the Buddha in the Punjab—Gandhara region.

In the *Janavasabha–Sutta* (No. 18) of the *Dīgha–Nikāya, Kurū* is mentioned along with the other *Janpadas* where *Tathāgata* delivered a number of religious discourses. According to the *Jātakas, Kurū* was 300 leagues in extent and Indapatta[6] (Indra–prastha, near modern Delhi) was its capital. "The ancient *Kurū* country, according to Dr. B.C. Law, may be said to have comprised the Kurukshetra or *Thāneswar*. The district included Sonepat, Amin, Panipat, Karnal and was situated between the Sarasvati on the North and Drishadvati on the South."[7]

Lord Buddha during His visits to the *Kurū* country generally stayed at *Kammasadhamma,* a market town of the *Kurū* people. The names of the *Suttas* delivered by the Buddha while at *Kammasadhamma* are as follows:—

(a) *Majjhima Nikāya* (Middle Discourses)

(i) *Satipatthāna Sutta*

Discourse (No. 10) on the Foundations of Mindfulness of the body, feelings, consciousness and mental objects. This *Sutta* is the basis of Vipassana meditation.

(ii) *Megandiya Sutta*

Discourse (No. 75) on abandoning sensual desires and craving, with Buddha's account of abandoning his life of pleasure in the three palaces. After this discourse, Megandiya, a noble of *Kammasadhamma,* was converted.

(iii) *Anajasappaya Sutta*

Discourse (No. 106) on the various ways of meditating on impassibility and the attainments, and on true release.

(b) *Digha Nikāya* (Long Discourses)

(i) *Mahā–Nidana Sutta*

Discourse (No. 15) on the Law of *Paṭiccasamuppāda,* the doctrine of Dependent Origination.

(ii) *Mahā–Satipattahāna Sutta*

Discourse (No. 22) is the same as Discourse No. 10 in *Majjhima Nikāya* i.e. on practising the Foundations of Mindfulness but with the commentary on the Four Noble Truths.

(c) *Samyutta Nikāya* (Kindred Sayings)

A discourse on the doctrine of Dependent Origination.

(d) *Anguttara Nikāya* (Gradual Sayings)

A discourse on ten noble states (*arriyavasa*).

Kammasadhamma, where the Buddha stayed during His Sojourn, and which is also mentioned in the *Mahasutasana Jātaka* and the *Jayaddisa Jātaka* as well as in the *Divyavadāna*[8], has not been identified by any scholar. We, however, propose to identify *Kammasadhamma* with Kaithal, a market town, 38 miles west of Karnal. In Sanskrit, its earlier name was Kapisthala[9], or the abode of monkeys. May be, the *Pāli* chroniclers changed its name to Kammasadhamma so that it may look dignified. More–over, according to a tradition, it was here that the man–eating ogre, Kammaspada was tamed and civilized by the Bodhisattva[10]. The proposed identification, therefore, seems to be reasonable.

Thullakotthita was another important town of *Kurū*–Desa. It received its name because of its grannaries. Here, after hearing a discourse of the Buddha, Ratthapala, a *Kurū* noble, had joined the Buddhist *Sangha.* His story and his true spirit of self–abnegation is narrated in the *Rattha–pala Sutta* (No. 82 of the *Majjhima Nikāya*). Now a days we are unable to find any town of that name in the *Kurū* country. In the Buddhist literature, Thuna or Sthuna is said to mark the Western boundary of the Buddhist Majjhimadesa (Middle country). As Hiuen Tsang's account makes Thaneswar the Western most country of the Buddhist Majjhimadesa, S.N. Mazumdar[11] has identified Thuna with Sthaneśwar or Thaneswar. Thaneswar is now a Tehsil head–quarters in the Karnal District. It is situated on the banks of Sarasvati and is a sacred place for the Hindus. Its name means 'the place of god' (Sthaneswara). Probably this Sthaneswara was the town referred to as Thulla–Kotthita (Sthulakoshita) in the *Pāli* Texts mentioned as the scene of the Discourse No. 82 of the *Majjhima Nikāya*. Here, Thullakotthita is mentioned as the capital of King Koravya of the *Kurū* Kingdom with whom Ratthapala (Rashtrapal) held a religious discussion.

That the Buddha had visited some other places in Punjab as well seems a possibility. According to a tradition which was popular during the reign of Asoka, Lord Buddha, while on a missionary tour of Punjab, had stayed at Srughna (modern Sugh near Jagadhri), at Kuluta (modern Kulu) and at Taki (modern Asrur in Gujranwala District, Pakistan). Further, in the last *bhanavara* or "the portion of tales" of the section on remedies in the *Vinaya* it is stated that the Buddha once went from Vaisali to Bhaddiyanagara and then returned to Savathi via Anguttarapa, Apana, Kusinara and Atuma. The same travel is related in the Tibetan version of *Vinaya* of the *Mula Sarvāstivādins* (Dul–va, III. 42 a). In his treatise 'Ancient People of the Punjab' Przyluski has identified[12] Bhaddiyanagara or Bhaddiya with Sakala (Sialkot) and Angutarapa with Agroha, an ancient city, 13 miles north–west of Hissar. In ancient days there ws a great route of commerce which passing through Sialkot, Agroha and Rohtak (Rohitaka) connected Taxila with the Gangetic Valley. The Buddha is said to have travelled by this route.

The Buddha may have visited Taxila also. Commentaries mention that in the Buddha's days also princes and other eminent men received their training at Takkasila[13] (Taxila) in Punajb. Pasenadi, King of Kosala, Mahali, Chief of the Licchavis, and Bandhula, Prince of the Mallas, were classmates in the University of Taxila. Jivaka, Dhammapala of Avanti, Kanhadinna, Bhardvaja and Yassadatta had also studied at Taxila. Jivaka, one of the foremost physicians of those days and a disciple of the Buddha was personally known to Puskarsari, the King of *Gandhāra*. Again, King Puskarsari (Pukkasati) was a contemporary and a friend of King Bimbisara of Magadha.

It is said that once King Puskarsari walked all the way from Taxila to Rajagriha to meet Lord Buddha. The Lord was at that time staying at Sravasti. On knowing the King's mission He hurried to Rajagriha and met Puskarsari at the hermitage of Bhaggava and delivered to him the *Dhatuvibhanga Sutta*[14]. From all this evidence it can be adduced that the Buddha was aware of the Gandhara region and had even admirers there.[15] Surely someone during the long period of 45 years must have invited Him to visit that country and He must have obliged His disciples including King Puskarsari.

On the basis of whatever little evidence is available at such a distant time, it is clear that the Buddha had sanctified the land of the five rivers. Thus the Punjabis were amongst the direct disciples of the Buddha.

References and Notes

1. According to tradition, the Buddha was born in 624–23 B.C. and attained *Mahāpari nirvāna* in 544–43 B.C. Some scholars opine that the Buddha was born in 567 B.C. and attained *Mahāparinirvāna* in 487 B.C.
2. Lumbini is in Nepal. just 10 km from the Indo-Nepalese border touching district Basti in Uttar Pradesh. Kapilavastu has since been identified with Piprahwa in District Basti in U.P.
3. As a mother who has borne a Future Buddha will never give birth to another child, *Mahāmāya* passed away after seven days. The child was, therefore, brought up by his stepmother Prajapati, who was sister of *Mahāmāya*.
4. *Vinaya Pitaka* Maha Vagga, I, Mahakhandhaka.
5. *Ibid.*
6. G.P. Malalasekera, *Dictionary of Pāli Proper Names*, 1960 edition. volume I, p. 641.
7. B.C. Law, *Geography of Early Buddhism*, 1932, pp. 17–18.
8. *Dictionary of Pāli Proper Names*, Volume I, p. 528.
9. *Imperial Gazetteer of India*. 1908, Volume XIV, p. 288.
10. *Dictionary of Pāli Proper Names*, Volume I, p. 529.
11. S.N. Mazumdar–*Introduction to Cunningham's Geography of Ancient India*, 1924, p. iii.
12. J. Przyluski, *Ancient People of the Punjab*, 1960 edition, p. 9.
13. *Dictionary of Pāli Proper Names*, Volume I, p. 982.
14. *Ibid.* Volume II, pp. 214–215.
15. It is worth noting here that in later years, the devotees of this region had by tradition imported Buddha to several places in Gandhara in order to add glory and sanctity to their beloved homeland.

ANNEX

Ratthapala Sutta
Majjhima Nikaya No. 82
(Abridged)

One of the prominent disciples of the Buddha, who showed a great spirit of self–abnegation, was Ratthapala, a Kuru noble. Once the Buddha was on a missionary tour in the Kuru country. He stayed at Thullakotthita, a town of the Kurus, in modern Haryana. When the inhabitants of this town came to know of the arrival of the Blessed One, they came to listen to the Buddha's discourse. Among them was a young man named Ratthapala (Rashtrapal), a scion of a leading family of the place. After the Buddha had finished His discourse and all others had gone, Ratthapala approached the Blessed One and showed his keenness to become a monk. The Buddha asked him to have the permission of his parents before adopting the life of a monk. Ratthapala went home and with great difficulty obtained the permission of his parents to join the Sangha and that too on the condition that 'he must come and see them occasionally'. Pomising to do so, Ratthapala went back to the Buddha and reported that his parents had since given him permission to become a Bhikkhu. Saying so, he sought admission to the fraternity of the monks. Admission was granted. Soon afterwards, the Buddha left for Sravasti. Ratthapala also accompanied.

Is a very short time Ratthapala became well–versed with the Dhamma and attained the stage of Arahatship. One day he approached the Buddha and sought permission for paying a visit to his parents. Scanning the thoughts of Ratthapala's mind and recognizing that he was incapable of abandoning his training and reverting to the life of a layman, the Buddha permitted him to go.

Then rising up and thanking the Lord, Ratthapala set out to visit his parents. Reaching Thullakotthita, he headed towards his father's house. At that time, his father was having his hair–cut. He saw the yellow–robed monk from a distance and started murmuring that these shaven–headed monks have snatched his son from him. And when Ratthapala came near him, he, without looking at him, abused the monk and forced him to return with the empty begging bowl. So, at his father's house, Ratthapala got nothing, but abuse.

On his way back, Ratthapala saw a maid–servant going to throw away some stale rice. He asked the maid–servant, "Sister, if you want to throw away this gruel, kindly put in into my bowl". As she was doing so, she recognised that the mendicant was none else but her master's only son. She rushed back and told Ratthapala's mother that her son has come back, and is just nearby. Overwhelmed by the news, Ratthapala's mother went to her husband, and asked him to go at once and bring their son for the meals.

Meanwhile, Ratthapala had gone out of the town and was taking his meal under the shade of a tree. When his father found him, he said: "Ratthapala dear, why are you eating stale porridge? "You could have come to your own home."

"Where, householders, is there a home for us who have gone forth from the home–life into homelessness? We are homeless ones. Of course, I did come to your house, householder, but I got neither alms nor polite refusal, only abuse I got."

Then, seeking pardon for the mal–treatment, his father said: "Come Ratthapala dear, let us go to the house."

"Not so, householder, I have taken my meal for the day," said Ratthapala. Then, his father requested Ratthapala to take next day's meal with them. Ratthapala agreed.

Next day, at the appointed hour, the venerable Ratthapala, duly robed and with begging bowl in hand, went to his father's house. Since his father wanted to entice him away from the monkish life, he placed a large heap of the family's wealth, gold coins and bullion, and pleaded with him 'to abandon his training and revert to the life of the layman', saying that if he will not revert to lay–life it will go waste as there was none else to enjoy it. But the venerable Ratthapala politely declined. Then, his father tried through Ratthapala's former wife to drag him into sensual pleasures but he remained firm and calm, and addressed her as sister. On being so addressed, she cried and fainted.

Then the venerable Ratthapala said to his father: "If there is food to be given, householder, then give it; do not harass me."

At last, the food was served, and Ratthapala came away after taking his meal.

Ven. Ratthapala then went to the King Koravya's Migacira Garden and sat down at the root of a tree to pass the day. While he was resting there, King Koravya came there. On knowing his identity, the King was very glad and with courteous greetings he asked him, "Master Ratthapala, men in this world renounce it for some kind of misfortune–illness, loss of property, wealth or family. But you have suffered no such thing, why you have renounced the world." In a calm and quiet manner, Ven. Ratthapala (Rashtrapala) replied, "Life in any world is unstable, is transient, is incomplete, is insatiate and the slave of craving." Then he summed up his philosophy of life in these words:

"I see men wealthy in the world who yet
Give not, from ignorance, their gathered riches
But greedily will hoard away their wealth,
Through longing for still further sensual pleasures.

A King who by his force conquered the earth,
And even lords the land the ocean bounds,
Is yet unsated with the sea's near shore,
And hungers for its further shores as well.

Most other men as well, not just a king,

Encounter death with craving unabated;
With plans still incomplete they leave the corpse;
Desires remain unsated in the world.

His relatives lament him, rend their hair,
Crying 'Ah me! Alas! Our love is dead!'
Then bear away the body wrapped in shrouds,
To place it on a pyre and burn it there.

Clad in a single shroud, he leaves behind
His property, impaled on stakes he burns,
And as he died, no relatives or kin
Or friends could offer refuge to him here.

While his heirs annex his wealth, this being
Must now arise according to his deeds;
And as he dies nothing can follow him;
Nor child nor wife nor wealth nor royal estate.

Longevity is not acquired with wealth,
Nor can prosperity banish old age;
Short is this life, as all the sages say,
Eternity it knows not, only change.

The rich man and the poor man both shall feel
(Death's) touch, as do the fool and sage alike;
But while the fool lies stricken by his folly,
No sage will ever tremble at the touch.

Better than wealth is widom, then,
By which the final goal can here be gained;
Fo, doing evil deeds in many lives,
Men fail, through ignorance, to reach the goal,

As one goes to the womb and to another world,
Renewing the successive round, so others
With no more understanding, trusting him,
Go also to the womb and to another world.

Just as a robber caught in burglary,
An evil–doer, suffers for his deed,
So people after death, in the next world,
The evil–doers, suffer for their deeds.

Sense–pleasures, varied, sweet, delightful,
In many different ways disturb the mind.
Seeking the peril in these sensual joys,
O King!I chose to lead the homeless life.

As fruits fall from the tree, so also men,
Both young and old, fall when this body breaks.
Seeing this too, I have gone forth, O King!
Better by far is the monk's life assured."

References and Notes

1. Source: The Wheel Publication No. 110, Buddhist Publication Society, Kandy, Sri Lanka, 1967.
2. Ratthapala was later included by the Buddha in the roll of foremost disciples (See *Anguttara Nikaya, Ekaka Nipata,* 'The Ones').

Chapter II

Aśoka The Great

When in 326 B.C. Alexander invaded India, he came into contact with various kings, notable amongst them being Ambhi of Taxila, and Porus who ruled the territory east of the Indus. Ambhi negotiated peace with Alexander and accorded him a rousing reception at his capital, Taxila. On the other hand, Porus met Alexander on the battle field. He was defeated but was reinstalled by Alaxender under dramatic circumstances. Thus, when Alaxender went back in 325 B.C. these two and other petty kings owed allegiance to the Greeks.

Soon after the death of Alexander in 323 B.C., the people of Punjab revolted against the authority of Mecedonia. Following the general confusion created by this upsurge, Chandragupta, a competent soldier and organiser, took advantage of the situation and captured the Greek garrison in the Punjab. Thereafter, with the assistance of some local chiefs in the Punjab, he defeated the last Nanda King of Magadha. Thus in 322 B.C. Chandragupta laid the foundation of the Mauryan Empire. The conquests of the Punjab and Magadha placed at Chandragupta's disposal the best army. With this huge and powerful army he extended the frontiers of his kingdom. When he died in 298 B.C. his kingdom extended from the Hindu Kush mountain to the Narbada.

Chandragupta was succeeded by his son, Bindusara, who ruled from 298 B.C. to 273 B.C. He conquered the Deccan and added it to the vast empire which he had inherited from his illustrious father. After Bindusara's death in 273 B.C. his son, *Aśoka,* ascended the Magadha throne. *Aśoka's* coronation took place after four years in 269 B.C.

Aśoka was fortunate in inheriting a well-established empire founded by his grand-father, Chandragupta. To this vast empire, *Aśoka* added Kalinga, modern Orissa, which he conquered after a bloody war. The large scale massacre in the Kalinga war deeply influenced the mind of *Aśoka* and brought revolution in his character. With this event, his outlook, both in his personal and public life, changed. Consequetly, he was drawn to the noble teachings of the Compssionate Buddha.

Impressed by the rational and humane teachings of the Buddha, *Aśoka* discarded the way of the force and declared his policy of victory through persuation. In pursuance of this policy of *Dhamma-vijaya* (Moral Conquest), *Aśoka* launched a concerted campaign to mitigate the suffering of the people, rather all living beings, in his empire. He undertook the provision of public works of utility on such a large scale which was never witnessed before in India. With a view to making travelling comfortable and safe, he planted shady trees on highways, dug wells and constructed rest house at appropriate places. He opened hospitals for men and animals alike. He also laid botanical gardens for the rare medicinal plants and healing shrubs (Rock Edict II). In order to improve the social conditions, *Aśoka* ordered abolition of sacrificial slaughter of animals: *samajas* (merry-making of a kind, accompanied by animal fights and feasting with consumption of meat etc.); hunting and other similar amusements (Rock Edict I). He devoted all his time and energy to the affairs of the State, and made arrangements to receive reports on State business at all hours. In Rock Edict VI, he says, "In times past, there was not before at all hours discharge of administrative business or the receiving of reports. So by me has thus been arranged, at all hours, when I am eating or in the harem, or in the inner apartments, or even in the ranches, or in the place of religious instruction, or in the parks, everywhere, *Prativedakas* are posted with instructions to report on the affairs of my people. In all places do I dispose off the affairs of the people"[1]. *Aśoka* thus spared no efforts for the weal and happiness of his subjects. He says,[2] "There is no greater duty for him than doing good to all." (Rock Edict VI). The benevolent *Aśoka* goes on to say, "All men are my children. I wish happiness and welfare to all men, as I would wish to my own children"[3] (Separate Rock Edict-Dhauli Text).

Aśoka toned his administration on the basis of the *Dhamma* tenets and emphasized the supermacy of the moral laws. To begin with, he commanded all his officers to tour the country-side at least once in five years for missionary work among the masses (Rock Edict III). Later, he created a separate Department of Missionary Service under the officers styled as *Dhamma-Mahamatras,* Ministers of Religion or Morals, for propagation of piety among his subjects (Rock Edict IV).[4] He also held regular religious conferences for preaching and discussing the *Dhamma;* and organised religious shows and processions (Rock Edict V). Further, *Aśoka* initiated his own pious tours or 'pilgrimages of piety' *(dhamma-yātrā)* to the sacred Buddhist shrines (Rock Edict VIII). *Aśoka* also opened *Dhamma* centres and endeavoured to popularise the practice of Buddhist meditation (*vipassanā*). And in order to preach and propagate the glorious doctrine of the Buddha in a systematic manner *Aśoka* sent missionaries to various territories and countries, both within and outside his kingdom. Amongst these pious missionaries were Majjhantika and Maharakkhita[5] who were commissioned to preach Buddhism in the Gandhara and Yona region (Greek settlements in North-West India) respectively. To supplement the efforts of the missionaries, *Aśoka* undertook, on a vast scale, the construction of the stupas and monasteries throughout his kingdom. He also issued a number of Pillar and Rock Edicts. In this compaign of *'Dhamma-Vijaya'* Punjab seems to have received special attention of *Aśoka.*

Hiuen Tsang, the Chinese pilgrim, who was in India from 630 to 644 A.D. saw the *Aśoka* stupas at the following, five places in Punjab, Haryana and Himachal Pradesh:

Palace	Indentification
1. Satadru	Modern Sanghol (Punjab).
2. Sathanesvara	Modern Thanesar (Haryana).
3. Srughna	Modern Sugh near Jagadhri (Haryana).
4. Kuluta	Modern Kulu (Himachal Pradesh.)
5. Tamsavana	Modern Sultanpur or Raghunathpur (Himachal Pradesh).

The selection of the sites for these stupas was not arbitrary. *Aśoka* raised these memorials at places which were traditionally connected with the life-events of Gautama the Buddha, in his past lives and the life-events of the past Buddhas. According to Hiuen Tsang:

1. The Stupa at Sanghol was near the place where the Past four Buddhas sat and walked.[6]
2. The Stupa at Thanesar contained 'relics of the Buddha and frequently emitted a brilliant light[7]:
3. The Stupa at Sugh was built by Asoka at the place where 'the *Tathāgata* preached the law to convert men.[8]
4. The Stupa at Kulu 'was a memorial of the traces of Buddha's visit to Kulu.[9]
5. The Stupa at Sultanpur was built near the site of the traces of the Past Four Buddhas where they sat and walked.[10]

As the seat of the Mauryan viceroyalty in Punjab was at Takshasila (Taxila), the Western Punjab now included in Pakistan, naturally claimed a major share of the Buddhist buildings built during the reign of *Aśoka.* Hiuen Tsang saw the *Aśoka* stupas at Narasinha (modern Ran-Si, 25 miles to the west of Lahore); Taki (modern Asrur in Gujranawala District)

Sakala (modern Sialkot); Manikyala (24 miles south-east of Taxila); and two stupas at Takshasila (modern Taxila).

Of all the *Aśokan* monuments in the Punjab, the most important was the Dharmarajika Stupa at Taxila. *Aśoka*, it appears, built this stupa over the body-relics of the Buddha which were allotted to Punjab after *Aśoka* opened the seven Stupas built over the holy relics by the contemporaries of the Buddha, and distributed the relics throughout his kingdom. Two relic caskets have since been discovered from the vicinity of the Dharmarajika Stupa.

Of the numerous Pillar Edicts issued by *Aśoka* at least one Major Pillar Edict was in the plains of Punjab. This pillar was at Topra, a village near Ambala from where it was removed by Feroz-Shah Tughlaq in 1356 A.D. to Delhi. It now stands on the ruins of Feroz-Shah Kotla, and is known as Delhi-Topra Pillar. The seven edicts on this pillar were inscribed in 243 B.C. and deal with the following subjects:

Edict	Subject
I	Exhortation of the practice of *Dhamma*.
II	What constitutes the practice of Dhamma.
III	Exhortation on vigilance against sin.
IV	The duties of the *Rajjukas*.
V	Prohibition of the killing of and infliction of pain on animals.
VI	*Aśoka*'s object in writing the Dhamma rescripts.
VII	Review of *Aśoka*'s life-long activities.

Out of the seven Edicts, the first six Edicts are similar to the Edicts inscribed on the Delhi-Meerut, Lauriya-Araraj, Lauriya-Nandangarh and Rampurva pillars but Edict No. VII is found only on this pillar and no where else. The seventh Edict on the Punjab Pillar is unique in the sense that it not only reviews *Aśoka*'s life-long activities for the weal and welfare of his subjects, but also throws valuable light on the ways and means adopted by *Asoka* for preaching and propagating the Noble Teachings of the Buddha. Inter-alia, the Edict says:

"Thus saith king Priyadarsi, Beloved of the Gods.

Whatever good deeds I have performed, those the people have imitated and to those they are conforming. Thereby they have progressed and will progress further in respect of obedience to mother and father, obedience to elders, courtesy to the *Brāhmanas* and *Śramanas*, to the poor and the distressed and even to slaves and servants.

This progress of Dhamma among men has been promoted by me only in two ways, *viz.* By imposing restrictions in accordance with the principles of Dhamma and by exhortation. But, of these two, the restrictions relating to Dhamma are of little consequence. By exhortation, however, *Dhamma* has been promoted considerably, The restrictions relating to *Dhamma* are, indeed, such as have been enjoined by me, *viz.* that certain animals are exempt from slaughter, and also the numerous other restrictions relating to *Dhamma* that I have imposed.

The progress of *Dhamma* among men has, indeed, been promoted by me considerably by exhortation in regard to the abstention from hurting any living being and abstention from killing any animal."

The creation of so many viharas, stupas and other monuments during the reign of *Aśoka* the Great gave a great fillip to the spread of Buddhism in the Punjab. In fact, the unprecedented activities in the cause of the *Dhamma* created a stir in the land of the five rivers which resulted in the advent of renowned Buddhist scholars and philosophers in the following centuries.

During the reign of *Aśoka* and immediately thereafter, there also flourished a local Buddhist kingdom in Punjab with Srughna, modern Sugh, near Jagadhri in the district of Ambala, as its capital city, and covering an area of about 1000 miles in circuit. Raja Dhanabhuti, the pre-eminent king of this royal family ruled from 240 B.C. to 210 B.C. This pious Buddhist king apart from building magnificent stupas in his capital city, also made munificent donations to the world famous Stupa of Bharhut in Central India which was constructed sometime between 250 B.C. and 200 B.C. According to an inscription discovered at Bharhut, Raja Dhanabhuti had borne the entire cost of the East Gateway of the Stupa. Most probably he was the donor of the other three gateways also. According to Cunningham, the inscription on the East Gateway reads as follows, after restoration:

"The ornamental gateway has been erected by the king of Srughna, Dhanabhuti, born of (the queen of) of the Vatsa family, (and) son of Aga-raja, born of (the queen of) the Gota family, (and) grandson of king (Visa Deva), born of (the queen of) the Gageya race, and spiritual merit has been gained (thereby),"[11]

Inspired by *Aśoka,* Raja Dhanabhuti also raised a number of stupas in and around his capital, Sugh. Hiuen Tsang, who visited Sugh in 635 A.D. saw there, besides an *Aśoka* Stupa, a number of stupas having body relics of the Buddha, Sāriputta and Moggallana-His two chief disciples, and other great *Arhats.* The ruins of one of these stupas have recently been dicovered, by Devendra Handa of the Kurukshetra University, at Chaneti, a small village situated about 3 km east of Jagadhri, and nearly the same distance north-west of Sugh or Srughna. According to him, the Chaneti Stupa was built during the reign of Raja Dhanabhuti. Summing up his observations, he says," Our Chaneti Stupa must have been one of those 'tens of topes' which were erected in Dhanabhuti's time in and around the capital city. The yellowish-red colour of the bricks which is typical of the Mauryan period and the plain, square and large-sized bricks 30 x 30 x 7 cms. corresponding with those used in the construction of the Bharhut Stupa lend further support to our surmise that this Stupa was erected sometime during the reign of king Dhanabhuti who ruled from 240 B.C. to 210 B.C."[12]

Raja Dhanabhuti was succeeded by his son, Vadha Pala in 210 B.C., and he in turn was succeeded by his son, Dhanabhuti

II, in about 180 B.C. That this royal family continued to donate liberally to the Buddhist shrines outside Punjab is evident from the two other inscriptions found at Bharhut and Mathura. According to the 2nd Bharhut inscription, the railings of that Stupa were the gift of Raja Dhanabhuti's son, Prince Vadha Pala. It says, "Dhanabhuti rajano putasa kumarasa Vadha Palasa (danam)."[13] According to the Mathura inscription, "the gift of Dhanabhuti II at Mathura included a *Vedika* or open building for reading, a Torana or ornamental gateway, and a Ratnagriha or treasury."[14]

References and Notes

1. Radha Kumud Mookerji, *Asoka,* Delhi , 1986 edition, pp. 144-145.
2. B.M. Barua, *Asoka* and *His Inscriptions,* Calcutta, 1968, 3rd Edition, Major Rock Edict, P. 246.
3. Sircar, *Inscriptions* of *Asoka,* Rock Edicts XV and XVI, pp. 56 and 59.
4. Sircar, *Inscriptions* of Asoka, p. 43.
5. *Māhavamsa,* XII, 1-8.
6. Samuel Beal, *Chinese Accounts of India-Travels of Hiuen Tsang-1957,* Volume II, p.21.
7. *Ibid.,* p.217.
8. *Ibid.,* p.218.
9. *Ibid.,* p.210.
10. *Ibid.,* p.218.

14. Alexander Cunningham, *The Stupa of Bharhut: A Buddhist Monument,, 1962 edition, p 129.*

12. Devendra Handa, *A Mauryan Stupa at Cheneti, an article* published in the *Vishvesh varanand Indological* Journal (Hoshiarupur) Vol. IV, Pt. (i); March, 1996.

13. Alexander Cunningham, *The Stupa of Bharhut,* 1962 edition, p.142.

14. *Ibid.,* pp.15-16.

Chapter III

Milinda and *Nāgasena*

After *Aśoka*'s death in 232 B.C., the wellknit Mauryan Empire began gradually to decline, partly due to the *Brāhmanic* reaction against it and partly due to the incompetency of the successors of *Aśoka*. The final blow to it was struck by the treacherous Pushyamitra Sunga, Army Chief of the last Maurya King Brihadartha, who assassinated his master in 184 or 185 B.C. and usurped the throne of *Pātaliputra*.

Soon after the collapse of the Mauryan Empire, Demetrius, a Bactarian Greek, invaded India, Demetrius was accompanied by two competent commanders, namely, Appllodotus and Menander. After conquering *Gandhāra* and Taxila, Demetrius is stated to have stayed back at Taxila but Appllodotus and Menander marched forward towards Ujjeni (Ujjain) and *Pātaliputra* (Patna) respectively. Menander reached and occupied *Pātaliputra* probably in 175 B.C. The occupation of *Pātaliputra* was, however, short-lived and Menander after his retreat from there made *Sagāla* (Sialkot) as his headquarters. Demetrius died in 166 B.C., and Appllodotus, who was a near relation of the King died in 161 B.C.

After his death, Menander carved out a kingdom in the Punjab. Thus from 161 B.C. onward Menander was the ruler of Punjab till his death in about 145[1] B.C. or 130[2] B.C.

The kingdom of Menander included *Gandhāra*, Sind and Punjab. In and around this territory, a large number of Menander's coins have since been discovered. *Sagāla* or Sakala (modern Sialkot), an old and historic city, was the capital of Menander. *Sagāla* is well-known in the Buddhist literature and has been mentioned in the oldest Buddhist Scriptures, namely, *Therigātha (Psalms of the Sisters)* and *Theragātha (Psalms of the Brethern)*. Hiuen Tsang here saw two stupas constructed by *Aśoka*, one of them commemorated the place where the Buddha is said to have stopped while on a missionary tour of Punjab.

Apart from being a competent soldier and warrior, Menander or Milinda was a scholar of distinction and was anxious to understand the essence of the religions of India, his new home. With this object in view, he approached many Indian teachers but none could satisfy his curious mind. So he was disheartened and exclaimed! 'All India is an empty thing, it is verily like chaff. There is no one capable of discussing things with me and dispelling my doubts". Under such circumstances, the King one day per chance saw a Buddhist monk, named *Nāgasena,*, passing nearby his palace. Milinda was very much impressed and attracted by the calm and serene personality of *Nāgasena,*. He summoned the monk to his court and questioned him about the religion to which he belonged. In a calm and scholastic atmosphere, this discussion commenced and lasted for many days. After *Nāgasena,* had solved a number of dilemmas and problems put by the King, Milinda became a Buddhist devotee. The record of the Dialogue between him and *Nāgasena,* is known as '*Milinda-Pañho*' It is divided into seven parts and contains 304 questions of king Milinda which cover almost all aspects of Buddhism. The *Milinda-Pañho (Questions of Milinda)* has the highest place in the non-canonical Buddhist literature.

After conversion to Buddhism, Milinda became an ardent champion of the Buddhist cause. He built a large monastery named *Milinda-Vihārā*[3] at Sialkot for the residence of Venerable *Nāgasena* and his colleagues. He also made substantial donations to the *Sangha* in other places. According to the Shinkot inscription, Milinda 'helped in the propagation of Buddhism.' From Shinkot in Bajaur (the frontier province of *Gandhāra* in those days) a relic casket[4] has also been discovered. This casket has an incription in Kharoshthi by the dedicator, an Indian Buddhist named Vijayamitra, who lived during the reign of Milinda. That Milinda was a devout Buddhist is further proved by some of his coins which bear the Wheel of Law *(Dharma-Chakra)*[5] of the Buddhists. After the disappearance of the Greek rule in about 100 B.C., Punjab was divided into small independent principalities or kingdoms of the local peoples. Important amongst them were: the Audumbaras, Trigartas, Kunindas, Yaudheyas and Arjunayanas. The Audumbaras ruled the country on the Upper Beas between Gurdaspur and Hoshiarpur districts with their capital perhaps near about Pathankot. The Trigartas ruled the area between the Ravi and Sutlej with Jalandhar as centre. The Kunindas had sway over the areas between the Sutlej (Ludhiana) and the Yamuna (Saharanpur) with their capital at Sugh near Ambala. The Yaudheyas ruled the territory southward of the Kunindas with perhaps Sonepat as centre.

Though we do not know much about others but it can be said with some certainty that the Audumbaras and the Kunindas were Buddhists. The Audumbaras find mention in the Buddhist Texts. In the Tibetan version of the *Vinaya* of the *Mūla Sarvāstivādins*, the capital of the Audumbaras is noted as the citadel of Buddhism in the north-western region. According to Przyluski, the Audumbaras had "attained a sufficiently high degree of culture and material prosperity before the beginning of the Christian era and were among the champions of Buddhism in the eastern region."[6] Some of the coins of the Audumbaras, which have been unearthed at Rupar, have the Buddhist stupa[7] embossed over them.

The Kunindas have been indentified by Cunningham with the royal family of Srughna (Sugh) by the line of Raja Dhanabhuti noticed by us in the previous chapter. His view is based on the coins of the king Amongabhuti[8], who calls himself as 'king of the Kunindas, which have been found in abundance around Sugh, particularly along the Upper Jamuna. The identification of the Kunindas is further supported by the discovery of the coins at Sugh of Aga-Raja, father of Raja Dhanabhuti I, and Raja Bala-bhuti who was most probably a later member of the same dynasty. The Kunindas have since been identified with the Kanets of the high hills of Himachal Pradesh, where, it is said, they were driven up by the advancing wave of immigration. According to Cunningham." the Kunindas or Kulindas, as the name is also written, are now represented by Kanets, who form nearly two thirds of the population of the hill tracts between the Bias and Tons Rivers. The name of Kunawar (Kinnaur) is derived from them; but there can be little doubt that Kunawar must have included the whole of Ptolemy's Kulindrine as the Kanets now number nearly 400,000 persons or rather more that sixty percent of the whole population between the Bias and Tons Rivers. They form 58 per cent in Kulu; 67 per cent in the states round about Simla, and 62 per cent in Kunawar (Kinnaur). They are very numerous in Sirmor and Bisahar (Bushahr) and there are still considerable number of them below the hills, in the districts of Ambala, Karnal and Ludhiana."[9] It is significant that a good number of Kanets in the districts of Kinnaur, Kangra (Kulu) and Lahul even to-day profess Buddhism.

References and Notes

1. W.W. Tran, *The Greeks in Bactaria and India,* 1951, p. 226.
2. A.K. Narain, The *Indo-Greeks,* 1957, p. 100.
3. P.V. Bapat (Gen.Ed.), *2500 Years of Buddhism,* 1956,
4. *The Greeks in Bactaria and India* op.cit., p. 520.
5. *Ibid.,* p. 407.
6. J. Przyluski, *Ancient Peoples of the Punjab,* 1960 edition, p. 9.
7. *The Greeks in Bactaria and India,* op.cit., p. 239.
8. Alexander Cunningham, *The Stupa of Bharhut; A Buddhist Monument,* 1962 edition, pp 16-17.
9. *Ibid.,* p. 17. Also see Cunningham's *Report of a Tour in the Punjab, 1878-79,* Vol. XIV, Archaeological Survery of India, p: 126.

Chapter–IV

Kanishka, A Kushana King

In about 80 B.C., *Sākās* appeared on the political scene of India. The first *Sākā* chief to invade and conquer a large part of Punjab and Gandhāra was Maues or Mauakes (in Kharoshthi, Mao or Moga). Maues, who later embraced Buddhism, was the first king in India to issue coins with the Buddha figure.[1] Maues died in 5 B.C. and was succeeded by Azes I. Thereafter, Punjab was for some time ruled by the *Sākā* Satraps, notable amongst them being Hagamasha, Hagana and Rajuvala or Rajula.

In the footsteps of the *Sākās*, came the Kushanas. The first Kushana chief was Kadphises I who, in about 25 A.C. occupied *Gandhāra* by displacing the last Greek King, Hermacus. As is evident from his coins discovered from Taxila, Kadphises I was a Buddhist. Apart from the Buddha figure, his coins bear the inscription[2] in Kharoshthi script '*Dharma–Thidasa or Sacca–Thidasa*' which means who is steadfast in *Dhamma* or true *Dhamma*. Kadphises I was the grand father of Kanishka who laid the firm foundation of the Kushana rule in India.

Prior to Kanishka, the Kushana rule was confined on the Indian side to *Gandhāra* only. In 78 A.C., however, Kanishka extended his kingdom upto Bihar in the east and upto Konkan in the south. Kanishka's capital was Purushapur, modern Peshawar. This great Buddhist king reigned from 78 to 101 A.C. Like *Aśoka*, Kanishka too undertook the propagation of Buddhism in India and outside India with the zeal and zest of a missionary. In other words, he completed *Aśoka's* work and helped in the triumphant spread of the *Buddha–Dhamma* throughout Asia. In the first century A.C. Buddhism in India was passing through a change. The literary activities of the distinguished Buddhist writers like Aśvaghośa, Vasumitra, and Pārsva were transforming it into *Mahāyāna*. Kanishka was attracted by the new form of Buddhism in the making. To give impetus to it, he convened the fourth Buddhist Council. The fourth Council was presided over by Vasumitra. *Aśvaghośa* was its Vice–President. Five hundred *Bhikkhūs* took part in the proceedings of this Council and arranged the doctrines of Buddhism and wrote commentaries in Sanskrit on them. The commentaries known as the *Vibhaśa Śāstras* covered all the three Piṭakas (Baskets) of the Buddhist Canon. According to Hiuen Tsang[3], the Council composed 100,000 stanzas of *Upadesa–Śāstras* explaining the canonical sutras, 100,000 stanzas of the Vinayavibhasa–sastras explaining the *vinaya*, and 100,000 stanzas of the *Abhidharma–vibhasasastras* explaining the *Abhidharma*. The *Mahāvibhāsa*, which is still preserved in Chinese, perhaps represnts the commentaries compiled by the fourth Buddhist Council.

As to where the Council convened by Kanishka was held is controversial. According to some it was held in Kashmir, while according to others it was held at the Kuvana monastery at Jalandhar (Jullundur). The Distt. Gazetteer states as follows: "The earliest historical mention of Jullundur occurs in the reign of Kanishka, the Kushana, who ruled from Kabul to the present U.P. There met, at his instigation, at Kuvana, near Jullundur about 100 A.C. a Council of Buddhist teachers, which set itself the task of collecting and arranging the sacred writings of Buddhism."[4] Hiuen Tsang who recorded in the 7th century A.D. the traditional account of Buddhism in India states that it was held in Kashmir. But the claim of Jalandhar as its venue seems to be well-founded. The account of this Council is found in many works composed much earlier than the Chinese pilgrim's visit. On that basis, eminent scholars like Dr. Radhakrishnan[5], Gurnwedel[6] and Wadell[7] have accepted Jalandhar as the venue of this Council. The authorities which maintain that it was held in Kashmir say that Jalandhar was first contemplated by Kanishka but was later on rejected on account of its heat and damping atmosphere. This is not a very valid reason for changing the venue as it could have been held during winter months. If at all the venue was changed later, it was probably shifted to Tamsavana monastery[8], where, according to Nando Lal Dey, the 4th Buddhist Synod was held. The Tamsavana convent was at modern Sultanpur or Raghunathpur at the confluence of Beas and Serheri. It is just about 25 miles northeast from Jalandhar city. The famous scholar Katyāyāna"[9], whose *Abhidharmajñana–Prasthana Śāstrā* was discussed by this Council, belonged to this monastery.

After this Council, Kanishka undertook systematic missionary work. Due to his intiative, guidance and patronage, not only Buddhism became more popular and deep rooted in the land of its birth but it was also successfully introduced into Central Asia and China. Also, the figures of the Buddha and the *Bodhisattvas* began to appear under the influence of the *Gandhāra* art.

Kanishka, like *Aśoka*, founded many monasteries, *chaityas* and stupas. Though the monuments created by him were scattered throughout his kingdom, the main stupas and *vihāras* were at his capital, Peshawar, at Taxila and in Kashmir. The Great Tope (Stupa) at Peshawar erected by Kanishka, was visited by Hiuen Tsang in 630 A.D. According to him, it was 400 feet in height, in addition to its base which was in five stages and 150 feet high. The ruins of this stupa have been identified with the ruins known as 'Shah–ji–ki–dheri' near Ganj Gate on the south–eastern out–skirts of Peshawar. The site was excavated in 1908–9 and one of the discoveries was the famous 'Kanishka Casket'. The casket which contained the holy relics of the Buddha was deposited by Kanishka himself. The reliquary has on its lid "a seated Buddha fllanked by two *Bodhisattvas*. In relief round the upper part of the cylinder is a frieze of flying geese; below is the main frieze with a figure of King Kanishka standing in front of an undulating garland supported by erotes and framing demifigures of votaries. On the lid and sides is a punctured inscription in Kharoshthi which twice mentions the name of Kanishka and concludes with the name of the master–mason: The servant Agisala, the overseer of works at Kanishka's *vihāra* in the *sangharama* of Mahasena"[10] This relic–casket is now the pround possession of Burma.

Kanishka must have raised religious buildings at other places like Jalandhar and Sialkot also but the spade of the archaeologist has not brought to light any such thing. Apparently, the buildings in these places were not so massive and magnificent and they could not withstand the ravages of time, weather and man.

The Kushana rulers continued to rule over North India upto the end of the 2nd century A.D. Important kings after Kanishka belonging to this royal house were. Kanishka II, Huvishka and Vasudeva. During their reign also the religion of the Buddha continued to flourish in the North-West region.

One of the greatest events in the history of Buddhism in India took place in the latter half of the 2nd century A.D. This was the constructon of the Great Maha Bodhi Temple at Bodh Gaya on the remains of the original temple built by *Aśoka.* Significantly enough, the Great Temple, which is standing even to–day, was built with liberal donaitons from Huvishka, the second successor of Kanishka. As an evidence"[11] for this historic event, we have an inscription at Bodh Gaya which records the construction of the Maha Bodhi Temple in the reign of Huvishka. The discovery of a gold coin of Huvishka amongst the relics deposited in front of the Vajrasana Throne, along with some silver punch–marked coins, also lends credence to this view.

References and Notes

1. W.W. Tarn, *The Greeks in India,* 1951, p. 400.
2. P.V. Bapat, *2500 years of Buddhsm,* 1956, p. 199.
3. Samuel Beal, *Chinese Accounts of India (Travels of Hiuen Tsang),* 1958, Volume II, pp. 193–194.
4. *Punjab District Gazetteers,* Volume XIV, Jullundur District, 1908, p. 22.
5. S. Radhakrishnan, *Indian Philosophy,* Volume I, 1951 edition, p. 584.
6. Grunwedel, *Buddhist Art in India,* p. 79.
7. Wadell, *Buddhism in Tibet,* p. 9.
8. Nando Lal Dey, *The Geographical Dictionary of Ancient and Medieval India,* 1927 edition, p. 202.
9. *Ibid.,* p.202.
10. Wheeler, *Five Thousand years of Pakistan,* 1950, p. 48.
11. Sir A. Cuningham, *Maha Bodhi or The Great Buddhist Temple at Bodh Gaya,* 1965 edition, pp. 2, 58.

Chapter–V

Asaṅga and Vasubandhu

After the collapse of the Kushana Empire towards the close of the 2nd century A.D., we enter upon a dark period in Indian history which continued till the rise of the Gupta Empire about two centuries later. The founder of the Gupta Empire was Chandragupta, who was originally a petty chieftain in Bihar but later on expanded his dominions to include the whole of Bihar and some part of Bengal. He proclaimed himself in 320 A.D. as *'Mahārājadhirāja'*, King of Kings. On his death in 330, Chandragupta was succeeded by his son, Samudragupta who ruled upto 380. Samudragupta exteneded his kingdom on all sides and included in it a large part of Punjab as well. Though a Hindu,Samudragupta had as his adviser the famous Buddhist saint and philosopher of Punjab, Vasubandhu. After his father's death, Chandragupta II succeeded Samudragupta and assumed the title of Vikramaditya 'Sun of Valour.' Vasubandhu continued to be his adviser also. Vasubandhu's association with this royal house was, it seems, helpful in bringing the Gupta Kings closer to Buddhism. Atleast two of the latter Gupta Kings were devout Buddhists. They were: Buddhagupta who succeded in 480 and Narasimhagupta or Baladitya who ascended the throne in about 500 A.D.

Asaṅga was the eldest brother of Vasubandhu. Both were born at Peshawar and educated in Kashmir. To begin with, both the brothers belonged to the *Sarvāstivāda* school of Buddhism which was dominent in the Punjab in those days. Later, in about 400 A.D. Asaṅga became a pupil of *Maitreyanātha*, the founder of the *Yogacāra* or the *Vijñanvāda* (consciousnes only) school. Afterwards Vasubandhu also became an admirer of this school.

Both Asaṅga and Vasubandhu were authors of distinction and they wrote masterly expositions on the Buddhist theories and practices. The most important works of Asanga were: 'The *Mahāyāna-samparigraha*; the *Prakarna-arvavaca*, the *Yogācarabhūmi-sāstra* and the *Mahāyāna-sūtralankāra*. The last two works are most important from the ethical and doctrinal points of view.

Vasubandhu's most important work was the *Abhidharma Kośa*, This grand work of 600 *Kārikās* proved invaluable for the propagation of Buddhism in India and abroad. In India, it was so popular that in the 7th century, *Bāna*, while describing the hermitage of the Buddhist monk, Divakaramitra, says, in *Harsha-carita* that, "Even some monkeys who had fled to the three refuges (the *Buddha*, the *Dhamma*, and the *Sangha*) were gravely busy performing the ritual of the *caitya*, while some devout parrots, skilled in the Sakya *Sāstraś*, were explaining the *Kośa (Abhidharma Kośa)*."[1] Yasomitra who wrote a commentary on Vasubandhu's *Abhidharma-Kośa*, says, that, on account of his spiritual attainments, Vasubandhu was known as a second Buddha by his contemporaries. "*Yam Buddhimatm agrayam dvitiya-miva Buddham ityahuh.*"[2] Besides the *Abhidharma-Kośa*, Vasubandhu wrote the *Paramartha-sartha-saptati*, an attack on the philosophy of the Sankhya teacher, Vindhyavasi, who was a contemporary of Vasubandhu According to Hiuen Tsang, Vasubandhu composed *Paramartha-saptati (Paramarthasatya Sāstrā)* while he was staying at Sakala (Sialkot)[3]. Vasubandhu also wrote commentaries on the *Saddharma-pundarīka Sūtra*, and *Mahāparinirvāna Sūtra* and the *Vajrac chedika prajañā-pāramīta*. His other works of distinction were on logic, namely, the *Tarka Sāstra* and the *Vāda Vidhi*.

That Buddhism was quite flourishing in the Punjab at the time Asanga and Vasubandhu lived has been testified by Fa-Hian, the first Buddhist pilgrim from China who was in India from 388–414 A.D. According to his estimates, there were at the time as many as ten thousand Buddhist monks in the Punjab. Summing up his observations, Fa-Hian says: "Here the Faith is very flourishing under both the Greater and Lesser Vehicles. When the people of the country saw Buddhist priests from China coming among them, they were much affected and said, "How is it possible for foreigners to know that renunciation of family is the essence of our religion, and to travel after in search of the Faith?" Then they gave to the pilgrims whatsoever they required, and treated them in accordance with the Faith."[4]

References and Notes

1. *Bāna, Harsha–Carita,* (Translated by E.B. Cowell & F.W. Thomas), 1961, p. 236.
2. P.V. Bapat, *2500 years of Buddhism,* p. 284.
3. Beal, *Travels of Hiuen Tsang,* Volume II, p. 206.
4. H.A. Giles, *The Travels of Fa-Hian,* 1956 edition, pp. 19–20.

Chapter–VI

Harsha, The Last Buddhist Emperor

The first half of the 6th century A.D. saw the disintegration of the Gupta Empire. Taking advantage of the slackening grip of the latter Gupta Kings, some of the local chieftains carved out Independent States. Two of such powers were, the Maukharis of Kanauj and the Vardhana dynasty of Thanesar. Kanauj or Kanyakubja (city of dwarfs) is in the Farrukhabad District of Uttar Pradesh and was on the right bank of the Ganges in its prosperous days. The river now flows at a distance of few miles to the east of Kanauj. Thanesar is now a Tehsil headquarters in the Karnal district of Haryana.

The first powerful ruler of the Vardhana Dynasty of Thanesar was Prabhakaravardhana (583–605 A.D.) who, to begin with, was a petty chief of the district of Sthanesvara (Thanesar) but became a powerful king by subduing the adjoining terriotires. As a result of his conquests in the four directons, Prabhakaravardḥåna was known as '*Māhārājadhirāja*' whereas his father Adityavardhana and grandfather Rajyavardhana I were simply called *Mahārājās*. Prabhakaravardhana had two sons, Rajyavardhana and Harshavardhana, and a daughter, Rajyasri. In the Madhuban inscripion, Rajyavardhana is described as a 'most devout worshipper of Sugata[1] (Buddha): Similar is true of both Harsha and Rajyasri as well.

In 605, while Rajyavardhana, eldest son of Prabhakaravardhana, was fighting in the battlefield against the Huns, the king passed away. Though Rajyavardhana was victorious, he returned home dejected due to the injuries and arrow wounds he received in the battle–field and disappointed due to the sudden demise of his father. Harsha and his elder brother were still mourning the death of their beloved father when suddenly a courier gave the tragic news of the assassinationof their brother–in–law, Grahavarman, the king of Kanauj, and the imprisonment of their sister Rajyasri at the hands of the Hindu king of Malwa. On hearing this sad news, Rajyavardhana rushed with his army to rescue Rajyasri.

Rajyavardhana was able to defeat the King of Malwa but he fell into a trap of Sasanka, Brahmin king of Gauda (Bengal), an ally of the Malwa king. He offered Rajyavardhana the hand of his daugther as a token of submission and friendship and called him to a meeting. When Rajyavardhana came to the meeting he was treacherously assassinated by the Gauda King. Thus, almost in quick succession Harsha, who was barely 16 at that time, lost his father, his brother–in–law and his brother. Not only that, the honour and life of his sister was also in peril. The young Buddhist prince, therefore, flared up and took a vow to punish the murderer of his brother and brother–in–law. So he rushed with his army to Kanauj. On the way, Harsha got the news that Rajyasri had been released and had entred the Vindhya forest. Hence, he changed his plans and turned to the Vindhya forest in search of Rajyasri. There he met by chance Bhikshu Divakaramitra, an old friend of the deceased Grahvarman. With his help, Harsha was able to trace Rajyasri when she was just going to end her life by mounting the funeral pyre. After rescuing Rajyasri, Harsha turned towards Kanauj. On reaching Kanauj, he found that Sasanka had in fear beat a retreat and the Malwa king had no courage to try strength. Thus he was able to retake Kanauj with ease.

Since there was no heir–apparrent to the Kanauj throne, Rajyasri, who had taken a vow to lead the life of a Buddhist nun, suggested and with the consent of the 'nobles of Maukhari court' Harsha was offered the crown. Thus Harsha became head of both the Thanesar and Kanauj royal houses.

After uniting the two kingdoms, Harsha, as says Hiuen Tsang, commanded his ministers, saying "The enemies of my brother are unpunished as yet, the neighbouring countries not brought to submission; while this is so, my right hand shall never lift food to my mouth. Therefore do you, people and officers unite with one heart and put out your strength."[2] Accordingly, they assembled all the soldiers of the kingdom, summoned the masters of arms. They had a body of 5,000 elephants, a body of 20,000 cavalry, and 50,000 foot-soldiers. He went from east to west subduing all who were not obedient. After six years he had subdued the Five Indies. Thus Harsha extended his hold over a vast territory including Punjab, Haryana, Uttar Pradesh, Bihar, Bengal and Orissa. This laid once again the foundation of Central power in North India. No wonder, Harsha was known as the Lord Paramount of North India (*Sakalotharaoathanatha*). Later, Harsha transferred his capital from Thanesar to Kanauj for administrative and political reasons.

Like *Aśoka*, Harsha devoted himself and directed all his power and pelf for the welfare of his people. He built *Dharmasālas* wherein arrangements were made to provide food, drinking water and medicines for the benefit of the poor and the sick. Hiuen Tsang says that Harsha "practised to the utmost the rules of temperance, sought to plant the tree of religious merit to such an extent that he forgot to sleep or eat. He forbade the slaughter of any living thing or flesh as food throughout the Five Indies on pain of death without pardon. He built on the banks of the river Ganges several thousand stupas; in the highways of the towns and the villages throughout India he erected hospices provided with medicines for travellers and poor persons, to be given without any stint."[3] In other words, Harsha devoted himself to the tasks of peace, the promotion of the material and moral interests of the country, and to bring out her cultural individuality and greatness.

Harsha ruled for over forty years from 606–647 A.D. and during this period Buddhism reached the zenith of glory. The flouishing condition of Buddhism in his empire is well illustrated by the data collected by Hiuen Tsang, the celebrated Chinese pilgrim, who was in India for about 14 years during Harsha's reign. According to him there were about over 100,000 Buddhist monks within Harsha's empire. Hiuen Tsang also tells us that India during Harsha's reign was extermely prosperous. Trade was brisk and people lived well. He adds that "the government is honestly administered, the criminal class is small, the people live together on good terms, are of pure moral principles, do not practise deceit, keep their obligations, and do not take anything wrongfully."[4] To quote the words of C.V. Vaidya, "The reign of Harsha was brilliant ending to the period that was passing; like a flame that bursts into brilliance before it expires, the condition of the country in the days of Harsha was flattering in every respect."[5]

Hiuen Tsang reached Peshawar in November 630 A.D. and stayed in India till July 644. Since Hiuen Tsang came by land route and went back also by the same route, he twice passed through Punajb. Peshawar, the capital of Kanishka, had greatly suffered from Huna invasions like many other places. Hiuen Tsang sadly notes: "Towns and villages are almost empty and abandoned, and only a few inhabitants are seen in the country. One corner of the royal town (Peshawar) contains about a thousand families. . . . There are about 1000 sangharamas which are deserted and in ruins." The Great Stupa of Kanishka was, however, still standing and the pilgrim gives a vivid account of the same. Hiuen Tsang also visited the mountain country of Uddyana (the Swat Valley) which had suffered more than Gandhara from the Huna inroads. According to the pilgrim, Uddyana had once 1,400 viharas and 18,000 Buddhist monks. On reaching Taxila, the pilgrim found "many monasteries in ruins with very few monks." From Taxila, Hiuen Tsang went to Kashmir where Buddhism still prevailed. Kashmir had about 100 monasteries with 5,000 monks. The pilgrim spent two years in Kashmir from May 631 to April 633 A.D., studying philosophy and having Buddhist sutras and sastras copied to take home with him to China. From Kashmir, he came to Punjab via Jammu, and reached Taki, the capital of Taki kingdom. From there, he went on 15 November 633 to Sakala (modern Sialkot) in Pakistan. There he saw a sangharama with about hundred monks of Hinyana persuation. He also saw three stupas still standing, two of them having built by Asoka–raja. From Sakala, Hiuen Tsang reached Chinapati, via Lahore or Kasur, the first major town in modern Punjab. We give below the chronology of his travels in ancient Punjab on the basis of the itinerary prepared bySir Alexander Cunnigham:

Date	Place
631 A.C.	
April 10	Taxila
June 15	Kashmir
633	
October 1	Leaves Kashmir
633	
November 10	Taki (Asrur)
November 15	Sakala or Sagala (Sialkot)
November 25	Lahore or Kasur
634	
January 1	Chinapati (Patti)
635	
March 15	Jalandhara
August 1	Kuluta (Kulu)
September 10	Satadru (Sanghol)
October 25	Sthaneswara (Thanesar)
November 1	Srughna (Sugh)
643	
September 20	Jalandhara
December 15	Taxila

Hiuen Tsang was a keen observer and has left for us very valuable account about the places he visited during his sojourn in India. Let us recapitulate what this scholar–pilgrim saw and noted about the condition of Buddhism in the area covered by modern Punjab, Haryana and Himachal Pradesh:

Chinapati[7]**:** This country is 2000 Ii in circuit. The capital is about 14 to 15 li round. . . . . The people are contented and peaceful; there are amongst them believers and the contrary. There are ten *sangharamas.'*

Comments[8]**:** From Sialkot, Hiuen Tsang came to Chinapati via Lahore or Kasur where he had stayed for one month. Chinapati (so known because it was the winter residence of Kanishka's Chinese hostages) has been indentified with modern Patti in Amritsar District. Here the pilgrim stayed for fourteen months, from January 634 to March 635 with a view to study *Abhidharma Śāstra* from a famous savant, Vinitaprabha[9], who had himself composed commentaries on *Pancaskandha–Śāstra* and *Vidyamatrasiddhi–Tridasa–Śāstra.*

Tamsavana[10]**:** To the south–east of the capital (Patti) 500 li or so, we come to the convent called Tamsavana. There are about 300 priests in it who study the doctrine of the *Sarvāstivāda* School. They have a dignified address and are of conspicous virtue and pure life. Three hundred years after the *Nirvāna* of Buddha the master of Sastras called Katyāyāna composed here *Abhidharma–jñana–prasthana–sāstra.*[10]

Comments: Tamsavana or 'Darkness wood' has been identified with Sultanpur in the Kulu Valley, situated at the confluence of Beas and Serhari. According to Cunningham, the whole of the western Doab–i–Jalandharpitha was covered with a thick jungle from which the monastery took its name. It is also called Raghunathpur. The monastery at Sultanpur must have been an important seat of Buddhism as *Aśoka* had invited some monks from here to participate in the third Buddhist Council held at *Pātliputra.* Around this monastery were innumerable stupas, and, according to Hiuen Tsang, some of them contained the relics of the Buddha. The scholar–monk Katyāyāna refered to by Hiuen Tsang flourished in the first century A.D. His work was discussed at the fourth Buddhist Council held under the aegies of Kanishka.

Jalandhara[11]: This Kingdom is about 1000 li form east to west, and about 800 li from north to south. The capital is 12 or 13 li in circuit. . . . . The people are brave and impetuous. The houses are rich and well supplied. There are fifty convents or so: about 2000 priests.

Comments: The city of Jalandhara visited by Hiuen Tsang in 635 A.C. was the modern Jalandhar. Even at that time it was a large city, 2 miles in circuit, and was the capital of the Jalandhara kingdom, also known as Trigartta. Apart from the modern district of Jalandhar, this kingdom also included the modern districts of Hoshiarpur and Kangra and the States of Chamba, Mandi and Suket The king of the Jalandhara kingdom was a Buddhist and an ally of Harsha. According to Hiuen Tsang, his name was Wu–ti–to (Wuddhi or Udito). Harsha was much pleased by his devotion to the *Buddha–Dhamma* and had given him sole control of matters relating to Buddhism even in his own kingdom. While at Jalandhar, Hiuen Tsang was treated as a State Guest by king Udito. When on his way back he passed through Jalandhar in 643 A.D. Harsha had charged king Udito to conduct the pilgrim in safety to the frontiers.

Of the 50 monasteries seen by our pilgrim, one was known as Nagardhana. Ven. Chandravarma[12] a famous Buddhist scholar, of those times resided in this *vihāra.* Hiuen Tsang stayed with him for four months and studied with him commentary known as *Prakarana–Pada–vidhasa–sāstra.* As already noticed Jalandhar was an important seat of Buddhism as early as the first century A.C. and, according to some sources, the Buddhist Council convened by Kanishka was held at Kuvana *Vihāra,* near this city.

Kuluta[13]: 'This country is about 300 li in circuit and surrounded on every side by mountains. The chief town is about 14 or 15 li round. . . The people are coarse and common in appearance. Their nature is hard and fierce. They greatly regard justice and bravery. There are about twenty *sangharamas* and 1000 priests or so.'

Comments: Kuluta is the modern city of Kulu and the areas around in the upper valley of the Beas river. In this valley is a celebrated place of pilgrimage, Trilokanath (Trailokyanath) situated on a hill in the village Tunda on the left bank of the Chandra–bhaga (Chenab) river It contains an image of Avalokitesvara[14] *Bodhisattva,* with six hands now worshipped as an image of *Mahādeva.* Lord Buddha is said to have come here and converted a Yaksha who later on built a monastery. In earlier times here was a stupa called the chi–chi–tope which contained a relic of the Buddha[15]. *Aśoka* had also erected here a stupa which was still intact when Hiuen Tsang visited Kulu in August 635.

Satadru[16]: 'This country is about 2000 li from east to west and borders on a great river. The capital is 17 or 18 li in circuit. . . . The manners of the people are soft and agreeable, the men are docile and virtuous. They all sincerely believe in the law of the Buddha and show it great respect. Within and without the royal city there are ten *sangharamas,* but the halls are now deserted and cold, and there are but few priests.'

Comments: Satadru was another name of the river Sutlej and in olden days also denoted a kingdom, the capital of which has been identified with, Sanghol near Sirhind. Here Aśoka had also constructed a stupa which was still standing at the time of Hiuen Tsang's visit.

Sthanesvara[17]: 'This kingdom is about 7000 li in circuit, the capital 20 li or so. The manners of the people are cold and sincere. The families are rich and given to excessive luxury. Most of the people follow after worldly gains, a few give themselves to agricultural pursuits. There is a large accumulation here of rare and valuable merchandise from every quarter. There are three *sangharamas* in this country with about 700 priests.

Comments: Sthanesvara (modern Thanesar) was the capital of the Vardhana Dynasty till Harsha transfered his capital to Kanauj. It is famous as the most sacred place in the holy land of Kurukshetra. Its name Sthanesvara means 'the place of god' or 'gods of the place'. It being the former capital of Harsha was an important seat of Buddhism as well. In addition to the *sangharamas,* there was an *Aśoka* stupa also which, according to our pilgrim, contained a peck measure of the relics of Buddha. About 20 miles to the south of the city was a famous monastery at the village of Gokantha or Govinda. This monastery had a succession of towers with overlapping storeys. According to Hiuen Tsang, the monks of this monastery were 'virtuous and well mannered, possessed of quiet dignity.'

Srughna[18]: 'This country is about 6000 li in circuit. On the eastern side it borders on the Ganges river, on the north it is backed by great mountains The river Yamuna flows through its frontiers. The capital is about 20 li in circuit, and is bounded on the east by the river Yamuna. It is deserted, although its foundations are still very strong. . . . . . The disposition of the people is sincere and truthful. There are five *sangharamas* with about 1000 priests. They deliberate and discuss in appropriate language (choice words) and their clear discourses embody profound truth. Men of different regions of eminent skill discuss with them to satisfy their doubts.'

Comments: Srughna has been identified with the village of Sugh, near Jagadhri, in Ambala District. Cunningham says, "The village of Sugh occupies one of the most remarkable positions that I have seen during the whole course of my researches. it is situated on a projecting triangular spur of high land, and is surrounded on three sides by the bed of the Jamuna, which is now the western Jamuna Canal, on the north and west faces it is further protected by two deep ravines, so that the position is ready made stronghold, which is covered on all sides, except the west, by natural defences."[19] Hiuen Tsang stayed at Srughna for about 4–5 months from November 635 A.D. onward. Here, in the company of Jayagupta[20] a famous Buddhist scholar of the time, the pilgrim studied the *Vibhāsa* of the Sautrantika School. The monastery in which Jayagupta resided was to the south–west of the capital and to the west of the river Yamuna. Outside its eastern gate was a stupa which was built by *Aśoka* to commemorate the Buddha's visit to this place. Nearby was another stupa which contained relics of the *Tathagata's* hair and nails. Two more stupas on the right and left of this stupa contained the hair and nail relics of Śariputta and Moggallāna, two famous disciples of the Buddha.

As is evident from the eye witness account of Hiuen Tsang, the religion of the Buddha was quite flourishing in the places visited by him from Taxila to Srughna (Sugh). In all, there were about 100 *Vihāras* and more than 5000 *Bhikkhūs* in the States of Punjab, Haryana and Himachal Pradesh. These facts and figures speak only of some of the places which Hiuen Tsang happened to visit. There might have been many more monks and monasteries in other places not visited by him.

For a number of years Hiuen Tsang was the guest of Harsha who treated the illustrious pilgrim with utmost reverence and hospitality. When Hiuen Tsang was about to leave India, Harsha convened a grand assembly at Kanauj to honour the distinguished guest. This assembly was attended by six thousand *Bhikkhūs* from all over India. At the site of this historic Conference, a hundred feet high tower was raised and on the top of it a golden image of Lord Buddha, equal to the King in stature, was kept. On this occasion, a grand procession was also taken out. After the Kanauj conference, Harsha took Hiuen Tsang to Prayaga (Allahabad) where he was holding his sixth quinquennial assembly. This grand display of charity or the *Mahā Moksha Parishad,* as it was called, commenced with the worship of Lord Buddha and lasted for seventy five days.

Harsha passed away in 647 after a glorious reign of about 42 years. With his passing away, Buddhism, which had seen great resurgence under his patronage, lost a great protector and benefactor; this hastened its decline and ultimate disappearance from India.

References and Nots

1. *Bāna, Harsha Carita,* (Translated by E.B. Cowell & F.W. Thomas), 1961 edition, preface, P. xi.
2. Hiuen Tsang, SI–YU–KI, *Buddhist Records of the Western World,* (Translated by Samuel Beal), In Two Volumes 1884, Reprint, Delhi, 1981, volume I, p. 213.
3. *Ibid.*, volume I, p 87.
4. *Ibid.*, p. 214.
5. Quoted in S. Natrajan and Mrs. Prema Radhakrishnan *Political and Historical History of India.* p. 247.
6. Sir Alexander Cunnigham, *Ancient Geography of India I,* Buddhist Period, 1963 edition, Appendix A, pp. 475–79.
7. Samuel Beal, *Chinese Accounts of India (Travels of Hiuen Tsang)* 1958–Volume II, p. 207.
8. Author's comments in all cases are essentially based on (i) Beal's *Buddhist Records of the Western World,* (ii) Watter's *'On Yuan Chwang's Travels in India',* (iii) Cunningham's *Ancient Geography of India,* (iv) B.C. Law's *Geography of Early Buddhism,* (v) Nando Lal Dey's *The Geographical Dictionary of Ancient and Mediaval India,* (vi) Surrendranath Sen's *India through Chinese eyes*'and (vii) *Imperial Gazetteer of India.*
9. *India through Chinese eyes, op. cit.* p. 23.
10. Beal, *Travels of Hiuen Tsang,* Volume II, p. 208.
11. *Ibid.*, pp. 209–210.
12. *India through Chinese eyes, op.cit.* p. 33.
13. *Travels of Hiuen Tsang, op.cit.* Volume II, p. 210.
14. *The Geographical Dictionary of Ancient and Mediaval India,* op.cit. 1927, p 106.
15. *'On Yuan Chwang's Travels in India, op.cit.* p. 299.
16. *Travels of Hiuen Tsang,* op.cit. Volume II, p. 211.
17. *Ibid.*, p. 215.
18. *Ibid.*, pp. 217–18.
19. *Ancient Geography of India, op.cit.* 1963 edition, p. 291.
20. *India through Chinese eyes, op.cit.* p. 34.

Chapter VII

Forgotten Creed

After the death of Harsha, India once again fell prey to anarchy and confusion. The Rajputs, a warrior class which had just come into being, took advantage of the disorder and disturbances in the country and made themselves masters of Northern India. They, thus, laid the foundation of many Independent States. The researches by modern scholars have shown that by and large the Rajputs are the descendents of the Parthians, Scythians, Huns etc., who invaded India from time to time and settled in this country permanently. Since they were nomadic tribes from Central Asia and possessed great martial spirit, the mild and gentle teachings of the Buddha did not appeal to their minds. The loss of the royal patronage, therefore, hastened the decline of Buddhism.

The Rajputs ruled over Punjab for about four centuries from 700 A.D. onward and this entire period was full of trouble and turmoil as throughout this period either the Rajput kings were fighting among themselves or were trying to prohibit the Muslim invaders from coming to India.

The Muslims intruded into Punjab in 977 A.D. under the leadership of Subuktgin, the ruler of Ghazani, who attacked the borders of Punjab, reduced certain forts and returned to Ghazani with a large booty. With the intrusion of the Muslims into Punjab, the final stage for the decline of Buddhism from the land of the five rivers was set in. Mahmud, who succeeded his father Subuktgin during his numerous raids plundered and destroyed whatever little remnants of Buddhism were left in this area. After his victory in the battle field in 1008,

Mahmud headed towards Nagarkot (modern Kangra) and plundered the famous Hindu and Buddhist temples[1] there on an unlimited scale. Mahmud came once again in 1011. This time he looted Thanesar, plundered its inhabitants, destroyed its historic temples and went back with a large booty. The Punjab was ultimately annexed to Ghazni by Mahmud in 1021. The Ghazni Dynasty continued to rule over Punjab through the Governors upto 1186 when Mohammad Ghori conquered it.

Unlike his predecessor, Mohammad Ghori came to conquer and retain the territory conquered. From that time onward, therefore, the land of the five rivers was continuously under the Mohammadan rule, though under different dynasties, till the Sikhs under the leadership of Maharaja Ranjit Singh became the masters of Punjab in the closing years of the 18th century.

With so many upheavels in the political field, the religion of the Buddha was bound to suffer and it did suffer to the maximum extent possible. As, however, no religion can disappear over-night the religion of the Buddha must have also lingered on in Punjab for a few centuries more after the fall of the Harsha Empire.

The fact that Buddhism was a living religion in some parts of Punjab till the 12th-13th, century is amply proved by the two inscriptions of Raja *Aśoka*-balla[2] or Asokachalla[3] dicovered at Bodh Gaya, the Seat of Buddha's Enlightenment, in Bihar. According to the first inscription. *Aśoka*-balla donated funds for carrying out some repairs to the Great Maha Bodhi Temple in the year 51 of the reign of Lakshmanasena, a King of Bihar. This would be 1251 A.D. according to Dr. A.S. Altekar and 1157 A.D. according to Cunningham. In this inscription, the last Punjabi Buddhist king, calls himself as the King of Sapadalaksha in the Punjab and pays his homage to the Buddha in these words:" Adoration to Buddha ! The Great *Śramana.* He it is who tells what the root is from which virtue springs, as also what it is that chokes that virtue. This is the virtuous gift of the great king, the illustrious Asoka-balla Deva, an adherent of the excellent *Māhayāna* School, a great *upāsaka* pious at heart. May, whatever be its merit, be for the advancement in spiritual knowledge, first of my father and mother, and after them of all beings."[4]

The territorial limits of the Sapadalaksha kingdom have not been identified so far by any scholar. The Sapadalaksha country is known as the earliest Himalayan tract to be inhabited by the Aryans. Cunningham equates Sapadalaksha with the Sawalak[5] (Siwalik hills) in the Punjab. The Siwalik range is a line of low hills (2000 ft. average elevation) as we go from Hoshiarpur in the Punjab plains towards Kangra Valley. In ancient days, the hill country between Beas and Sutlej and the Jalandhar Doab was known as Jalandhara or Trigarta. In the 7th century A.D. when King Wuddhi (Udito) was ruling the Trigarta country, Jalandhar city was its capital. After the Muslim onslaught in about 1000 A.D., however, the territory of the plains was lost and Kangra became the capital of the hill province[6]. Raja Asoka-balla appears to have regained the plains of Doab and added to the hill province[7]. So the Sapadalaksha kingdom may have atleast covered the Jalandhar-Hoshiarpur-Kangra-Mandi complex, with possibly Kangra (Nagarkot) as capital. As we know, Nagarkot or Kangra was for a long time a stronghold of the *Māhāyana* Buddhists in the Punjab. Significantly enough, Raja Asoka-balla also declares himself as' an adherent of the Excellent Mahayana School'.

Some light on the condition of Buddhism in the Punjab in the 13th century is also thrown by the travel accounts of the Tibetan pilgrims, who came to Punjab (Jalandhar-Pitha) to pay their homage to the second *Nāgar-juna* (600-650 A.D.), the founder of Vajrayana.

Of the numerous Tibetan pilgrims, the most important ones were: 'Orgyan pa and his master Godts' an pa. The pilgrim Orgyan pa, who undertook his pilgrimage most probabley after 1250 A.D. has left for us a brief but interesting description about the Jalandhara country *i.e.* the territory between the

Sutlej and the Beas, including the Kulu valley. His travel account runs as follows:—

"The country which is very big is called Dsva lan dha ra, but it has numberless towns; Naga ko te means in Tibetan" The castle of the snake'. He stopped in that place for about five months. But since the nourishment was scanty and agreeable food was lacking, his body was in a very bad condition. Then he returned to Tibet. Avoiding the route he took formerly, he went by a short-cut since he wanted to visit the holy place of Kuluta. After two days along that route he met in a place called ki ri ram a great ascetic called Anupama whom he asked for the explanation of the law. The other uttered 'Homage to the Buddha, Homage to the *Dhamma,* Homage to the Community' thus bestowing upon him the protection of the three jewels, and then he added; "we both are two Vajrabrethren disciples of Acharya Nagarjuna. Go to Tibet you will greatly benefit the creatures".

"Then he went to the holy place *(tirtha)* of Kuluta which corresponds to the knees of the body included in the circle of the *(Vajra) kāyā* as represented by the twenty-four holy places. The core of this place is called *Siddhi* where there is a forest of white lotuses in flower; there, upon a stone are the foot-prints of Buddha. In that place one reaches quickly the best powers of the common degree, but one meets also many hindrances; in this place there are two venerable *(bhadanta)* and one yogin".[8]

Another Tibetan traveller whose travel account is available was Stag Ts' an Ras pa. He says :

"Then we went to Jalandhara. At that place there is a great town called Nagarkete (Nagarkot), in a river there is triangular piece of land, digging the soil there is forbidden, there is a cemetary called Lan gura where there is a boulder which looks like a skull; a self-made image of Aryabhattarika appears there. To the north, there is a famous image called *Javālāmukhi* where on looking at the divine face everything blazes in fire. Near the royal palace there is a cemetary called Mitapara where there is a cave of the Mahatma Nagarjuna called Mitagulr. In the proximity, there is a warm rock which is said to have been the meditation hut of *Nāgarjuna*".[9]

Nothing is known about Buddhism and its votaries in the land of the five rivers after the 13th century. Thereafter, it was completely forgotten in the whole of Punjab except in the high Himalayas where, because of the flow of Buddhistic ideas from Tibet, it continued to flourish and is even to-day a living faith.

References

1. S.M. Latif, *History of the Punjab, 1964 edition,* pp. 82-83.
2. Sir A. Cunningham, *Mahabodhi or the Great Buddhist Temple at Bodh Gaya, 1965 edition,* pp. (iii) & 78.
3. Dr. A.S. Atekar, *Introduction to Biography of Dharmasvamin, A Tibetan monk* (translated by Dr. George Roerich) 1959, pp. xvi-xvii.
4. *Mahabodhi or the Great Buddhist Temple,* op.cit. pp. 78-79.
5. *Ibid.,* pp. 78-79.
6. *The Imperial Gazetteer of India,* Vol. XIV, 1908, p. 383.
7. Ct. *Introduction to Biography of Dharma-svamin,* op. cit. p. xviii.
8. G. Tucci, *Travels of Tibetan Pilgrims in the Swat valley,* 1940, p. 25.
9. *Ibid.,* op. 43.

Chapter VIII

Some Archaeological Remains

Punjab, being the border State, had always been the hunting ground of the invaders who came one after the other in large numbers. These hordes of successive armies from abroad plundered, damaged and destroyed the historical buildings to such an extent that they could not withstand for long the ravages of time, weather and man.

Pakistan

Taxila is the only place in the greater Punjab which has yielded Buddhist antiquities covering a continuously long period of more than 800 years, that is, from the time of *Aśoka* the Great till Taxila met its tragic fate at the hands of the savage Huns in the 5th century A.D. of the numerous Buddhist remain discovered at Taxila and other places in Pakistan, the important ones are described here in brief :

1. **Dharmarajika Stupa**. Of all the stupas discovered at Taxila, the Dharmarajika Stupa is the most significant and the oldest. This stupa has been nicknamed Chir (Split) Tope by the archaeologists because of 'a wider cleft which former treasure seekers drove through its dome. It was first built by *Aśoka* over the body relics of the Buddha who is also called '*Dharmaraja*', the Lord of the Law. These relics were discovered by Sir John Marshal in 1913–14 from a nearby chapel where they appear to have been re-enshrined by a Bactarian Buddhist. The text in the Kharoshthi characters on the golden reliquary containing the relics reads as follow :

"In the year 136 of Azes, (A.C. 78), on the 15th day of the month of A*shadha,* on this day relics of the Holy One

(Buddha) were enshrined by Urasaka, Scion of Imtavhria, a Bactrian, resident of the town of Noacha. By him these relics of the Holy One were enshrined in his own *Bodhisattva* chapel at the Dharmarajika stupa at Takshasila, for the bestowal of health upon the great king, king of kings, the son of Heaven, the Kushan; in honour of (his) parents, friends, advisers, kinsmen, and blood-relations; for the bestowal of health upon himself. May this thy right munificent gift lead to *Nirvāna.*[1]

These relics were handed over by the Government of India to the Maha Bodhi Society of India, and are now enshrined in the Mulgandha Kuti Vihara at Sarnath, the Holy Isipatana.

All round the Dharmarajika, numerous small stupas, chaples and *sangaramas* have come to light. Apart from the relics mentioned above, a bone relic of the Buddha was discovered from another stupa. These relics were presented by the Government of India in 1917 to the Buddhists of Sri Lanka and were enshrined by them in the Temple of the Tooth (Dalada Maligawa) at Kandy[2].

2. Kalawan monastery : The Buddhist establishment at Kálawan, about one and a quarter miles to the south-east of the Dharmarajika, is the second largest at Taxila. Amongst the innumerable shrines here was a relic chamber which was found intact. A copper plate discovered from this chamber has the following inscription in Kharoshthi characters :

"In the year 134 of Azes, (A.C. 76), on the twenty–third day of the month of *Sravana,* on this date Gandrabhi, the female worshipper (*Upāsikā*) daughter of Dharma, the householder (*grahapati),* wife of Bhadrapal, establishes relics in Chadasila, in the stupa shrine together with her brother Nandivardhana, the householder together with her sons Sama and Sacitta and her daughter Dharma, together with her daughters-in-law Raja and Indra, together with Jivanadin, the son of Sama, and her teacher in acceptance of the *Sarvāstivādas,* having venerated the country–town; for the veneration of all beings; may it be for the obtainment of *Nirvāna*".[3]

3. Jaulian monastery : The original shrines at Jaulian are on the top of a hill and belong to the Kushana period. The famous Jaulian monastery which was found highly ornamented, however, belongs to a later period. On the northern gate of the main stupa at Jaulian, is seated Buddha with an ex-voto inscription recording that it was the gift of one Buddhamitra,[4] who 'delighted in the law (*dhamma*)'. Among the many other small stupas have been found the figures of the Buddha and *Bodhisattva,* and a relic chamber as well. One of the stupas contains a number of donative inscriptions. One inscription reads *'Sanghamitrasa Buddhadevasa bhikshua danamukho'*[5]. The pious gift of *bhikshu* Buddhadeva, friend of the *Sangha.* The Jaulian monastery has one of the best preserved group of stucco figures. In its centre is seated the Buddha in the attitude of mediation (*dhyana-mudra),* with a standing Buddha to his right and left and two attendant figures. Of the latter, the one to the left carries the fly-whisk *(chauri),* the other is the Vajrapani holding the thunderbolt in his left hand'[6].

4. Kunala Stupa

The Kunala Stupa was identified by Marshal with the stupa over the ridge of Hathial which commands the whole of the Hare Valley.

The story of Kunala, as recorded by Hiuen Tsang, is very interesting. Kunala was son of the great Buddhist emperor Asoka Maurya. His step-mother Tishya-rakhshita fell in love with him and induced Asoka to send him as his Viceroy to Takshasila. Disappointed in love, she sent orders that the eyes of Prince Kunala may be removed. For these orders she used the seal of the king which she secured when he was asleep. The ministers of Kunala shuddered at the orders and shrank from its execution but the obedient son forced them to do their job. His eyes were put out and he along with his wife begged his way to the capital Pataliputra where Asoka recognized him by his voice and the strain of his flute, and on knowing the facts put the demonic wife to death. The eyes of Kunala were, later, restored at Bodh Gaya through the good offices of Arhat Ghosha.

The stupa now identified to commemorate this story stands on a rectangular base of 63 feet 9 inches in width and 105 feet in length. Nothing but a fragment of the core of the superstructure has survived but this little portion combined with the 3 terraces gives a fair idea of the time of its erection. A number of architectural pieces of the superstructure which are lying around at the base help one to conclude that the elevation of the dome and drum was strikingly lofty, and that it was a circular tower rising in six or seven tiers. It is also very clear that the terraces and different tiers were decorated with friezes and cornices.

5. Mohra Muradu

This stupa lies about a mile to the south-east of Sirsukh. It is a beautiful stupa with high edges, surrounded by dark green shrubs.

When excavated, it was found that the whole of the structure upto the top of the dome was covered with images of Buddhas and Bodhisattvas in close succession one upon the other. The stucco reliefs are coloured, though all the colour has now faded. The art, as seen on the stupa, reaches a very high standard of excellence. The figures, particularly on the bays of the south side of the plinth, have been endowed with life and movement. In the words of Marshal, "this life and movement is specially evident in some of the attendant Bodhisattvas, the swish of whose robes, with the lines delicately contoured beaneath them, is wornderfully true and convincing. Delicate too, and figures which emerge from the background at the sides of the Buddhas as if they were emerging from the clouds.

6. Charsada and Pushkalavati

Charsada is the most important of the sites so far discovered or excavated in the Gandhara region. As already mentioned, Pushkalavati was one of the oldest centres of ancient civilization. It was an ancient city even for the people of Buddha's time. Before the discovery of the Khyber pass the trade from India to Balkh and Bakhtar (Bactria) was carried through the defile created by the Kabul river. Charsada was the first business centre that greeted the Central Asian caravans heading for this sub-continent and was an equally important centre of export from this country.

Buddhist Jatakas added to its importance by declaring it to be the seat of the Bodhisattva who in his different births gave the gift of his flesh, his eyes and even of his head.

These remains have suffered the most disastrous destruction at the hands of nature. The Swat river which according to the Jatakas, had obeyed the command of the Blessed One and had stopped its annual scourge, has forgotten the pledge and has cut the regular mound of the remains into four pieces. Its current has already washed away most of what would have been a source of valuable information.

7. Takhte Bahi

Takhte Bahi is another important Buddhist shrine. The main group of buildings at Takhte Bahi stand on a small plateau over five hundred feet above the surrounding plan. The big stupa is a huge building within a large court. It has a cross-court full of votive stupas, a monastic quadrangle, monastic cells and a huge assembly hall. To the south of the quadrangle is another court which was decorated by a line of gigantic Buddhas rising to a height of 16 to 20 feet. The most remarkable in design and arrangement is a group of small shrines surrounding the main stupa court which are alternatively crowned with stupa-like decorations and gabled chaityas. The beauty and grandeur provided by the entire composition is unparalleled in the Buddhist world.

8. Sahre Bahlol

Like Takhte Bahi, Sahre Bahlol has also been discovered recently after a complete oblivion of some fifteen hundred years. The city was probably founded by Kushana kings and finally reduced to debris by the fire and sword of Mihiragula, the Hun worshipper of Siva. The excavators have dug out more than half a dozen large monasteries, burnt and laid low.

But the destroying fire has proved a wonderful preserver. The fall of the superstructure entombed the lower buildings. Human hands never reached them afterwards. The rows of $4^1/_2$ feet high Bodhisattvas on both the sides of the great stupa and the stucco base of the smaller stupa are still in magnificent condition of preservation.

The images both in stucco and stone show a wide range of craftsmanship but all of them have a very high standard of excellence and represent the Gandhara Buddhist art at its best.

9. Asokan Rock Edicts

Two Major Rock Edicts of Asoka have been discovered in Pakistan. These are at Shahbazgarhi, near Mardan, in Peshawar district, and at Mansehra in Hazara district in North-West Frontier Province. These were discovered in 1836 and 1889 respectively. The contents of these Edicts are the same as in other places, and they contain all the Fourteen Major Rock Edicts issued by Asoka.

Punjab

The modern States of Punjab, Haryana and Himachal Pradesh are practically devoid of any archaeological remains. No traces are now available of the numerous Buddhist monasteries which were seen by Hiuen Tsang as late as the 7th century A.D., at Jalandhar, Patti, Kulu, Thanesar and Sugh. However, some idea of their glory and grandeur can be had from the marvellous art and architecture of the monasteries discovered at Sanghol.

The recent excavations at Sanghol in Tehsil Samrala, Distt. Ludhiana have brought to light the rich heritage of Buddhism in Punjab. The name Sanghol has originated from Sanghpur-town of Buddhist monastic nature. Sanghol is 65 km from

Ludhiana and 40 km from Chandigarh on the Ludhiana-Chandigarh road. Sanghol is 16 km by road from Sirhind railway station. Another nearby railway station is Morinda, 9 km from Sirhind-Nangal loop Line.

The most important monument unearthed on 2nd February 1985 at Sanghol by the experts of the Department of Archaeology and Museums, Punjab is the stupa and the monastery complex. The Stupa, which appears to have been first built by Asoka in the 3rd century B.C., is on the pattern of *Dharma-Chakra* (Wheel of Law). The cylindrical stupa is of 16 metre diameter on a 17 metre square platform-the *pradakashina* or circumambulation of the stupa raised at height. There is also a *surkhi* or *murram* pathway about 5.34 m in width all around the stupa. In the east is paved pathway along which a number of votive stupas of solid mud were erected by the devotees.

From the central portion of the stupa were recovered a tooth, ashes, and some bones as also the bottom portion of a relic casket-most probably the body relics of the Buddha. The excavations also yielded a lid with a Kharosthi legend of 1st-2nd century B.C.Upasaka Ayabhadra mentioned in the legend may have been responsible for enshrining the relics in the stupa.

The priceless find at Sanghol,[7] which has put it prominently on the archaelogical map of India, is the discovery of 117 sculptures of the Kushana period from the railing around the stupa on the square platform. These railing pillars were found in a pit between the monastery and the stupa on February 2, 1985. The valuable parts of he railing include 4 corner pillars, 58 upright pillars, 7 double-sided pillars, 35 cross bars and 13 coping stones.

Of the four corner pillars, one is with *Dharma-chakradhvaja*, two with *Simhadhvaja* and the last with stupa and devotees. The upright pillars have beautiful carvings of *Yakshis*, an *Upāsaka* (a lay devotee), a *Chakravartin* (a royal devotee). The coping stones mounted on the railing pillars are decorated with a series of arched windows containing Buddhist symbols like *dharmachakra,* lotus, worship of the relic casket, worship of Buddha's bowl and other auspicious symbols. The cross bars which join the two pillars are decorated with lotus medallions. The Sanghol sculptures are considered as the best specimen of the Buddhist art of 2nd century A.D.

During the excavations in the adjoining areas, a broken portion of stone from a gateway of the stupa, depicting *Jātaka* stories, in redstone, was also recovered. Coins of all the kings of the Kushana dynasty and also seals and sealings in Kharosthi and Brahmi scripts have been discovered. A large citadel with internal and external moats has also been unearthed. The monastery is yet to be fully excavated.

Some other Buddhist remains found in Ludhiana District are at Tihara, a place in the north-west corner of Jagraon Tehsil. Tihara has been identified with the city of Varat mentioned in the *Mahabhārata.* On the mounds here a large number of small square copper coins have been found having on one side the Buddhist[8] wheel and on the other the names of the Rajas in old Sanskrit. Besides coins, impressions of seals in burnt clay, large bricks, dice glazed pottery and many other antiquities, including the impressions of coins of the Yaudheyas in clay have also been found. Another place important from Buddhist point of view in this Tehsil is Arura, which lies a little north of Bhader and about 10 miles south of Jagraon, "The old tank called Raniyana near Arura is frequented by numerous pilgrims. People say that the ancient name of this place was Ahichatta, and that its ruler, Raja Buddhamati, composed a work in Prakrit, entitled *Dharma Kathā,* which is still used by the Puja tribe in the District"[9].

Haryana

In the Bhivani Tehsil of Hissar District, there is a small hill named Tosham, just 16 miles to the south of Hissar. Its summit is surmounted by an ancient fort. There is a Sanskrit inscription on a rock on the face of the hill. Is seems to refer to a Scythian King, Tushara, who appears to have conquered the Gupta Golotkacha who reigned form 50-79 A.C. there is evidence to show that the Tosham hill had a Buddhist monastery. The date of inscription is said to be A.C. 162-244.[10]

At Theh Polar, 10 miles north of Kaithal in Karnal District, also some evidence of Buddhism[11]" has been observed by way of Indo-Scythian coins unearthed there. At Chaneti, about 3 k.m. east of Jagadhri, the ruins of a Mauryan Stupa[12] bulit during the reign of Raja Dhanabhuti of Sugh (240–210 B.C.) have been discovered recently. Another recent discovery in *Haryana* is the image of the Buddha of the 4th-5th century discovered at Ghraura, a village in the District of Gurgaon.

Himachal Pradesh

In the Kangra District, close of Pathiar, 6 miles south-east of Kanihara, 4 miles from Dharmsala on Chanru river, two rock votive inscriptions in Brahmi and Kharosthi have been discovered which record the foundation of Buddhist monasteries[13] in the 2nd century A.D. during the regin of the Kushana kings. A much later inscription (of 5th of 6th century) found at Cheri, a village 8 miles east of Nagarkot, contains the Triple-Gem formula of the Buddhists. The ruins of a large Stupa, circumference of which is more than 800 feet, have also been discovered at Chetru, situated at a distance of 5 miles east of Nagarkot (Kot Kangra).[14]

At Rewalsar, 15 miles from Mandi, there is an old shrine dedicated to Padmasambhava[15] who was an Indian teacher and went to Tibet in 747 A.D. to propagate Buddhism. This *Manipāni* temple is believed to have been constructed at the spot where Padmasambhava meditated.

The Major Rock Edicts of Asoka have been found at seven places in India. One of them is at Kalsi, near the confluence of Yamuna and Tons rivers at Paonta in district Sirmur of Himachal Pradesh. This was discovered in 1860.

The contents of these Edicts are the same as in other

places, and they contain all the Fourteen Major Rock Edicts of Asoka. In brief, the contents of the fourteen Major Rock Edicts are as follows :

Edict No. Subject

I. Abolition of

(a) Sacrificial slaughter of animals.

(b) Samaja (merry-making of a kind, accompanied by animal fights, feasting with consumption of meat etc.)

(c) Slaughter of animals for royal table, except two peacocks and one antelope.

II. (1) Provision of works of utility, viz :

(a) Hospitals for men and beasts.

(b) Botanical gardens for the culture of medicinal plants, indigenous and foreign (obtained by import), including "herbs, roots and fruits".

(c) Wells and trees on the roads for the comfort of travellers and animals.

(2) Supply of medical aid and facilities in foreign countries, and in countries on the borders.

The countries specificially mentioned are the South Indian Kingdoms and Sri Lanka as well as the Greek king Antiyoka i.e. Antiochus II Theos, king of Syria and West Asia.

III. Institution of quiniquennial tours of officials for the propagation of the Dhamma.

IV. Success attained by his propagation of the Dhamma through religious shows and processions is greater than that attained by conventional methods. Asoka adds that as a result of the practice of Dhamma by him, the sound of the drums has become the sound of the Dhamma.

V. Appointment of Dhamma-Mahamatras–ministers of

Religion of Morals, for propagation of piety among his subjects (including royal relations), as also among foreign people.

VI. Asoka's tireless zeal in serving the interest of the public. "there is verily no duty which is more important to me than promoting the welfare of all men [16]". says Asoka.

VII. Asoka's impartiality towards all religious sects. He wishes that all sects everywhere should live harmoniously, and achieve self-control and purity of mind.

VIII. Commencement of Dhamma tours, and abolition of "Tours of pleasure" accompanied by "hunting and other similar amusements".

IX. Asoka says[17], "Many of the ceremonies performed are corrupt and useless. Such ceremonies are considered by me of small or no result. But there is one ceremony which bears great fruit, namely, the ceremony of the Dhamma; kindness towards slaves and servants, respect to teachers, are meritorious In living beings, self-control is meritorious; almsgiving is meritorious. The almsgiving declared meritorious is thus : not the giving of alms but the giving of the Dhamma; the promoting of the Dhamma".

X. The object of Asoka's exertions to spread the Dhamma. Asoka "does not consider[18] either glory in this life or fame after death as of great consequence, except in regard to the following, viz. that the people of his dominions would practise obedience to Dhamma and also that they would act in accordance with the principles of Dhamma".

XI. Asoka says[19]. "There is no such gift as the gift of Dhamma, no such act of dividing as the separation of Dhamma from what is not Dhamma, and no such kinship as kinship through Dhamma".

XII. The desirability of inter-communal understanding and regard. Asoka says[20], "the growth of the essentials of Dhamma among men of sects is possible in many ways. But its root lies in restraint in regard to speech, which means that there should be no extolment of one's own sect or disparagement of other sects on inappropriate occasions and that it should be moderate in every case even on appropriate occasions".

XIII. After expressing his deep regret and remorse for the misery and suffering caused by the Kalinga war, Asoka "makes amends[21] for the suffering he himself has caused and wishes security for all beings. He considers that self control, impartiality and cheerfulness are important but the chief of victories is conquest through the Dhamma". Asoka also lists here various parts of his dominions, countries on the borders, and the foreign countries where the Dhamma was taught by his messangers.

XIV. A review of the Rock Edicts. Asoka says[22] that "In the series of records, there are texts written in a concise form, or in a medium form, or in an elaborate form. And all the items of the series have not been put in all places. There are some topics which have been repeated over and again owing to their sweetness, so that people may act accordingly".

Delhi

As we have seen, the story of the archeological remains in Pakistan, Punjab, Haryana and Himachal Pradesh begins with *Aśoka,* the first Buddhist Emperor. So also is the case with Delhi. In fact, the Capital of India has the best *Aśoka* heritage. *Aśoka* is said to have erected 84,000 Stupas, Monasteries and *Vihāras.* He also issued a number Edicts (royal proclamations) through the medium of rocks and pillars. In these Edicts he preached the fundamental principles and practices of *Dhamma* or moral life so that the people may adopt the Buddhist way of life.

The Edicts of *Aśoka* have since been discovered at 36 places within the boundaries of modern India. Of these, three Edicts-two Pillar Edicts and one Rocks Edict-are in Delhi. The two pillars were brought to the imperial city in the 14th century but the Rock Edict is an original gift of *Aśoka* to the capital of India. The discovery of this Edict shows that Delhi was an imporant centre of Buddhism at the time of Asoka.

Delhi Rock Edict

The *Aśokan* Rock Edict in the capital was per chance noticed in March 1966 by Jang Bahadur Singh, a contractor, when it was about to be blasted away for the development of a colony. It lies on the top of little hillock to the southeast of Delhi at Bahapur, on the south of Srinivaspuri and west of modern Kalkaji Temple. The location of this Edict suggests the existance of highway as alluded to in the *Pāli* literature wherein it is stated that Indapatta was linked by straight road with Varanasi.

According to scholars, who have translated the inscription, the Delhi Edict represents the shorter version of the Minor Rock Edict of *Aśoka,* almost similar to the one found at Bairat (Rajasthan). The language of the inscription is Prakrit, akin to those of the Delhi-Topra and Delhi-Meerut Pillar Edicts. The text of the Delhi Rock Edict is as follows :[23]

"Thus saith the Beloved of the Gods.

A little more than two years and a half have passed since I am avowedly a lay follower of the Buddha. But I was not vigorously exerting myself in cause of *Dhamma* for the first one year. However, it is a little than a year that I am devoutly attached to the *Sangha* and exerting myself vigorously.

The gods, who were unmingled with the people inhabiting Jambudvipa during the ages down to the present time, have now been made by me mingled with them. This is indeed the result of my exertion in the cause of *Dhamma.*

And this result is not to be achieved only by the people of superior position like myself; but even a poor man is as well able to attain the great heaven if he is zealous in the cause of *Dhamma.*

Now, this proclamation has been issued for the following purpose, *viz.* that both the poor and the rich may exert themselves., that even the people residing in the territories outside the borders of my dominions may realize this, and that this exertion on the part of the people may be of long duration. This cause will be made by me to progress more or less to one and half times".

Delhi-Topra Pillar

This pillar was removed by Sultan Feroz Shah Tughlaq in 1356 A.D from Topra, a village near Ambala, and re-erected at Ferozabad, now known as Feroz Shah Kotla. The height of this pillar is 42 feet 7 inches. How this pillar was transported to Delhi makes an interesting reading. It is said that it was brought on a special carriage with 42 wheels. With each wheel a rope was fastened which was pulled by 200 men. Thus about 8400 men were deployed to fetch this pillar from a distance of about 120 miles.

All the seven Edicts on this pillar were issued by Aśoka in 243 B.C. The six Edicts are similar to the other Major Pillar Edicts but the seventh Edict (No. VII) is found only on this pillar and nowhere else. The Delhi-Topra Pillar was first identified as an Asokan Pillar by Captain Polier in 1785. The text of the seven Edicts on this pillar is as follows.[24] :

No. I

"Thus saith king Priyadarsi, Beloved of the Gods.

This record relating to *Dhamma* has been caused to be written by me twenty-six years after my coronation.

Happiness is this world and in the next is difficult to secure without intense love of *Dhamma,* rigorous self-examination, implicit obedience to elders, great fear of sin and excessive zeal in the cause of *Dhamma.* But verily owing to my exhortation, this yearning for *Dhamma* and love of *Dhamma* have increased and will further increase among my people day by day. And my officers, whether of the superior, inferior or middle rank, are conforming to the practices of *Dhamma* and practising the duties associated with *Dhamma* and they are capable of stirring up others to do the same The Mahamatras in charge of the bordering districts are also acting in the same way For these indeed are the rules for them, *viz.* governing the people according to *Dhamma,* administering justice to them according to *Dhamma* and protecting them according to *Dhamma.*

No. II

Thus saith king Priyaḍarsi, Beloved of the Gods.

The practices of *Dhamma* are meritorious. But what does *Dhamma* consist of? It consists of the least amount of sin, many virtuous deeds, compassion, liberality, truthfulness and purity.

Even the gift of eye-sight has been bestowed by me in various ways on criminals threatened by punishment. To bipeds and quadrupeds as well as to birds and aquatic animals have I done various kinds of favour even upto the grant of life. And many other virtuous deeds have also been performed by me.

This record relating to *Dhamma* has been caused to be written by me on stone for the following purpose, *viz.,* the people may act according to it and that it may endure for a long time And he, who will act thus, will do what is meritorious.

No. III

Thus saith king Priyadarsi, Beloved of the Gods.

A person has an eye on his good deed only and says to himself : 'This good deed have I done'. Not in the least does he notice his sin, saying to himself : 'This sinful act have I perpetrated', or This indeed is what is called sin'. But this is certainly difficult to scrutinize. Nevertheless, one should verily look into the matter thus : 'These passions surely lead to sin, such as violence, cruelty, anger, vanity and jealousy. Let me not ruin myself by reason of these very passions. One should seriously reflect on the following : 'This one is for my good only in this world and the other one is for my good also in the next world'.

No. IV

Thus saith king Priyadarsi, Beloved of the Gods.

This record relating to *Dhamma* has been caused to be written by me twenty-six years after my coronation.

The Rajjukas have been placed by me over many hundred thousands of persons among the people of my dominions. The award of rewards or the imposition of punishment by them has been placed by me under their sole control. Why? Because the Rajjukas should perform their duties with confidence and without fear and they should bring welfare and happiness to the people of the country side and bestow favour upon them. They will acquaint themselves with what gives pleasure or pain to the subjects and exhort the inhabitants of the countryside through persons who are devoted to *Dhamma,* so that the people can attain happiness in this world as well as in the next.

Of course, the Rajjukas are eager to serve me. They have also to obey the officers who know my wishes. And these officers will exhort some of the Rajjukas who may not know my wishes, so that the latter can please me.

Just as a person feels confident after having entrusted his child to an experienced nurse and thinks : 'This expert nurse is able to bring up my child well', even so have I appointed the Rajjukas for the welfare and happiness of the country-people. The award of rewards or the infliction of punishment by the Rajjukas has been placed by me under their sole control in order that they should be fee from fear and want of confidence and thus perform their duties with pleasure.

The following indeed is desirable, *viz* that there should be impartiality in judicial proceedings and impartiality in punishment. And my order goes even so far that a respite of three days is granted by me to fettered persons in the prisons, who have been convicted and condemned to death. During that period, their relatives will plead for their life to some officers. Otherwise, they will console the persons who are going to die and bestow gifts in order to secure for them,happiness in the next world and undergo fasts for the same purpose. Verily, my desire is this that, even when the time for their living in this world has expired, they may attain happiness in the next world and that various kinds of the practices of *Dhamma,* such as self-control and distribution of gifts, are promoted among the people.

No. V

Thus saith king Priyadarsi, Beloved of the Gods.

Twenty-six years after my coronation. I have declared the following species of animals exempt from slaughter, *viz.* parrots, mainas, ruddy geese, wild geese, nandimukhas, gelatas, bats, queen-ants, terapins, boneless fish, vedaveyakas, gangapuputakas, skate-fish, tortoises and porcupines, leaf-hares, twelve-antler stags, bulls set at liberty, household vermin, rhinoceroses, white pigeons, village pigeons and all the quadrupeds which are neither useful nor edible.

Those she-goats, ewes and sows, which are either pregnant or milch, are not to be slaughtered, nor their young ones which are less than six months old. Cocks are not to be caponed. Husks containing living beings should not be burnt. Forests must not be burnt either uselessly or in order to destroy living beings. The living must not be fed with the living.

At the three *Chaturmasis* and at the fullmoon of the month of *Tishya* for three days in each case, *viz.* the fourtheenth of one fortnight and the first of the next, and invariably on every fast day, fish is exempt from slaughter and should not be sold. And on the same days, not only these but also other species of beings should not be killed in the elephant forests and in the fishermen's preserves.

On the eighth of each fortnight and on the fourteenth and fifteen, on the Ti*shya* and *Punarvasu* days, on the three *Chaturmasis* days and on every auspicious day, bulls are not to be castrated. And he-goats, rams, boars and such other animals as are usually castrated should not be castrated on those days. Horses and bullocks should not be branded on the T*ishya* and *Punarvasu* days, on the *Chaturmasi* and during the fortnights associated with the *Chaturmasis*.

Upto the time when I complete twenty-six years after my coronation, the release of prisoners has been ordered by me for twenty five times during the period in question.

No VI

Thus saith king Priyadarsi, Beloved of the Gods.

Tweleve years after my coronation, records relating to *Dhamma* were caused to be written by me for the first time for the welfare and happiness of the people, so that, without violation there of, they might attain the growth of *Dhamma* in various respects.

Thinking : "In this way only the welfare and happiness of the people may be secured, "I scrutinize as to how I may bring happiness to the people, no matter whether they are my relatives or residents of the neighbourhood of my capital or of distance localities. And I act accordingly. In the same manner, I scrutinize in respect of all classes of people. Moreover, all the religious sects have been honoured by me with various kinds of honours. But What I consider my principal duty is meeting the people of different sects personaly.

This record relating to *Dhamma* has been caused to be written by me twenty-six years after my coronation.

No. VII

Thus saith king Priyadarsi, Beloved of the Gods.

Those kings, who flourished in times past had this desire : 'How can the people progress through the promotion of *Dhamma*? But the people did not progress through an adequate promotion of Dhamma.

Thus saith king Priyadarsi, Beloved of the Gods, on the point.

This thought occurred to me: 'In time past, kings desired as to how the people could progress through an adequate promotion of *Dhamma*. The people, however, did not progress through an adequate promotion of *Dhamma*. How can the people progress assuredly through as adequate promotion of *Dhamma*? How can I elevate them through the promotion of *Dhamma*'?

Thus saith king Priyadarsi, Beloved of the Gods, on this point.

This thought occurred to me: 'I will cause proclamations of *Dhamma* to be proclaimed and instructions in *Dhamma* to be imparted. Hearing these, the people will conform to them, will be elevated and will progress considerably through the promotion of *Dhamma*'.

For this purpose have I caused proclamations of *Dhamma* to be proclaimed, and various kinds of instructions in *Dhamma* have I ordered to be imparted, so that those officers of mine, who are placed by me over many people, will also preach and dis-seminate them. And the Rajjukas are placed by me over many hundred thousands of beings and they have also been ordered : 'Instruct the people who are devoted to *Dhamma* in such and such a manner'.

Thus saith Priyadarsi, Beloved of the Gods.

Having this very matter in view, I have set up pillars bearing records relating to *Dhamma,* appointed *Mahamatras* to deal with the affairs connected with *Dhamma* and issued proclamations on *Dhamma*.

Thus saith king Priyadarsi, Beloved of the Gods.

Banyan trees have been caused to be planted by me on the roads, so that they will offer shade to beasts and men Besides mango–groves have been caused to be planted by me for the same purpose And I have caused wells to be excavated at intervals of eight Krosas, and rest-houses have also been caused to be constructed by me. Moreover, numerous watering sheds have been caused to be set up by me at different places for the enjoyment of beasts and men. This provision of enjoyment is, however, certainly a trifle. Because mankind has been blessed with many such comforts by former kings as well as by myself. But I have done this for the following purpose, *viz.* that people might conform to such practices of *Dhamma.*

Thus saith Priyadarsi, Beloved of the Gods.

Those *Dharma-Mahamatras* of mine are occupied with varius kinds of activities which are beneficial both to ascetics and o house-holders. And they are occupied with all the religious sects. I have arranged that some of them will be occupied with affairs of the *Sangha* Likewise I have arranged that some of them will be occupied with the *Brāhmanas* and Ajivikas. Similarly I have arranged that some of them will be occupied with the *Nirganthas.* In the same way I have arranged that some of them will be occupied with various other religious sects. The different *Mahamatras* are occupied especially with the affairs of the different religious sects. My *Dharma-Mahamatras* are occupied not only with the communities referred to above but also with all the other sects not mentioned specifically.

Thus saith king Priyadarsi, beloved of the Gods.

Those mentioned above and many other chief officers of mine are occupied with the delivery of the gifts of myself as well as of the queens. And to all the members of my entire household, they are bringing, in various ways, reports regarding the worthy recipients of gifts both here and in all the quarters. And I have arranged that some of the officers shall be occupied with the delivery of the gifts of my sons and of other queen's sons, so that the noble deeds of *Dhamma* and the practice of *Dhamma* may be promoted. My intention is that the noble deeds of *Dhamma* and the practice of *Dhamma,* which consists of compassion, liberality, truthfulness, purity, gentleness and goodness will thus be promoted among men.

Thus saith king Priyadarsi, Beloved of the Gods.

Whatever good deeds I have performed, those the people have imitated and to those they are conforming. Thereby they have progressed and will progress further in respect of obedience to mother and father, obedience to elders, courtesty of the *Brāhamanas* and *Sramanas,* to the poor and the distressed and even to slaves and servants.

Thus saith king Priyadarsi, Beloved of the Gods.

This progress of Dhamma among men has been promoted by me only in two ways, *viz.* by imposing restrictions in accordance with the principles of *Dhamma* and by exhortation. But, of these two, the restrictions relating to *Dhamma* are of little consequence. By exhortation, however, *Dhamma* has been promoted considerably. The restrictions relating to *Dhamma* are, indeed, such as have been enjoined by me, *viz.* that certain animals are exempt from slaughter, and also the numerous other restrictions relating to Dhamma that I have imposed.

The progress of *Dhamma* among men has, indeed, been promoted by me considerably by exhortation in regard to the abstention from hurting any living being and abstention from killing any animal.

For the following purpose has this lithic record been prepared, *viz.* that it may last as long as my sons and great grandsons shall reign and the moon and the sun shall shine and also that the people may conform to it. If a person conforms to this, happiness in this world and in the next will be attained by him.

This record relating to *Dhamma* has been caused to be written by me twenty-seven years after my coronation.

Saith the Beloved of the Gods on this point.

This record relating to *Dhamma* should be engraved on stone tablets, wherever they are available, in order that it may endure for a long time".

Delhi-Meerut Pillar

This pillar too was brought to Delhi by Sultan Ferozshah Tughlaq. It was brought in 1360 A.D. from Mirath, a village near Meerut, and erected in his royal palace on the Ridge, Delhi. During 1713-19, it was broken into five pieces due to the explosion of a powder magazine. In 1750, the inscriptions on this pillar were discovered by Padre Tieffenthaler.

In 1838, it came into the possession of Hindu Rao, a Maharashtra nobleman. He presented it to the Asiatic Society of Bengal. The inscribed portion was, therefore, sawed off and sent to Calcutta. In 1866, the inscribed portion was returned by the Society, and a year later, in 1867, all the pieces were joined together and the completed pillar erected in the present position by the British Govt. Its height is 32 3/4 feet.

The Delhi-Meerut Pillar has practically the same text of the first six Edicts found on the Delhi-Topra Pillar.

References and Notes

1. Sir John Marshall, A Guide to Taxtila, 1960 (fourth edition), *pp.* 113–14.
2. *ibid*, p. 106.
3. *ibid.*, p. 134.
4. *ibid.*, p. 166.
5. *ibid*, p. 167.
6. *ibid.*, p. 167.
7. S.P. Gupta (Ed.) *Kushana Sculptures from Sanghol* -Ist-2nd Century A.C., Volume I,
8. *Punjab District Gazetteer*, Ludhiana District, 1904 Volume, XV A., p. 14.
9. *ibid.*, p. 14.
10. *ibid.*, Hissar, 1915 Volume IIA, part A, p. 256.
11. *ibid*, Karnal, 1918 Volume VI A, p. 14.
12. Article by Devendra Handa, *Vishveshvaranand Indological Journal* (Hoshiarpur) Volume I Part (i) (March 1964).
13. *Punjab District Gazetteer*, Kangra, 1904, Volume XA, Part A. p. 249.
14. *ibid.*, p. 258.
15. *ibid.*, Mandi State, 1920. p 17.
16. D.C.Sircar, Inscriptions of Asoka, Delhi, 1957, p. 45.
17. A.A.G. Bennet, the Asoka Inscriptions, The Maha Bodhi Journal, November-December 1963, p. 286.
18. Sircar, Inscriptions of Asoka, p. 55
19. *Ibid.*, p 49.
20. *Ibid.*, p. 50.
21. A.A.G. Bennet, The Asoka Inscriptions, The Maha Bodhi, November-December 1963, p. 287.
22. Sircar, Inscriptions of Asoka, p. 55.
23. *Journal of the Royal Society of Britain and Ireland*, parts 3 and 4, 1967-Article by M.C. Joshi and B.M. Pande, A Newly-Discovered Inscription of Asoka at Bahapur, Delhi.
24. Dr. D. C. Sircar, In*scriptions of Aśoka*, pp. 67-77.

2. Ibid, p. 156
3. Ibid, p. 154
4. Ibid, p. 156
5. Ibid, p. 155
6. Ibid, p. 157

9. Ibid, p. [illegible]

15. Ibid, [illegible] 1923, p. 17

19. Ibid., p. 56
20. Ibid., p. 59

Chapter IX

Revival and Survival

I. Delhi

Delhi stands on the site of the celebrated Indraprastha which is said to have been founded by the *Pāndvas.* During the time of the Buddha, Indraprastha (Pali : Indapatta) was a flourishing town in the Kuru country. In the *Kurudhamma Jātaka,* Dhanajaya Koravya is mentioned as its King. Delhi seems to have been associated with Buddhism from the earlist period, as according to a verse found at the end of the *Buddhavaṁsa,* Buddha's razor and needle were enshrined at Indapatta.

According to a tradition, Raja Dillu founded Dilli (Delhi) in about 400 B.C. upon the site of Indraprastha. Chandragupta Maurya, who founded the Mauryan Empire in about B.C. 322, included Delhi in his empire. His grandson, Asoka (B.C. 273-232), was the first Buddhist king to rule Delhi.

When the Mauryan Empire crumbled in B.C. 187 Delhi passed on to Hindu rulers, notable among them being Vikramaditya of Ujjain who conquered it in B.C. 57. Delhi again came under the Buddhists when Kanishka (78-101 A.D.), the most important ruler of the Kushana Dynasty, included it in his empire. The last Buddhist King to rule Delhi was Harsha (606-647 A.D.) of the Vardhana Dynasty of *Thānesar.*

The first ruler to make Delhi his capital was Anangpal, a Rajput Chief of Tomar clan, who came from Kanauj and built his capital in A.D. 1052. He was followed by Prithvi Raj (1164-1192 A.D.) who was killed in a battle with the Turks at Tarauri in 1192. From then onward the Muslims ruled Delhi, the last being the Moghuls who ruled till its annexation by the British in 1857. Under the British, Delhi was till 1911, one of the five administrative divisions of Punjab. On 12 December 1911, however, the King Emperor George V at a Royal Durbar in Delhi proclaimed that thence-forth Delhi, in place of Calcutta, would be the capital of India. Thus in 1912, Delhi was carved out as a separate unit and made the capital of modern India.

By the time India gained Independence in 1947, the great Buddhist heritage, its art and culture had been brought to light to a great extent by the archaeologists, explorers and scholars. When the Constitutent Assembly was busy in drafting a Constitution for free India, the question of the National Flag and the National Emblem baffled the founding fathers. Their eyes ultimately turned towards the Buddhist heritage which represented the glorious past of India.After careful consideration, the Constituent Assembly adopted unanimously the Buddhist Wheel of Law (*Dharmachakra*) and Lion Capital of the Asoka Pillar at Sarnath as the National symbols of free India. Accordingly, the *Dharmachakra* which appears on the abacus of the Sarnath Lion Capital of Asoka, became the central part of the National Flag of India on 15 August 1947. The Lion Capital of Asoka, which also symbolises Buddhism, became the National Insignia on 26 January 1950 when India became a Sovereign Democratic Republic. On the same day, the Viceroy House, the citadel of the British Viceroy, became the seat of the President of India. In the Durbar Hall of Rashtrapati Bhavan, as it is now known, where the imperial durbars were held during the British rule with the Viceroy seated in the silver coronation chair, now stands a tall meditative 5th century A. D. Buddha as if to bless the rulers of modern India.

Buddhism came to life in the capital of India in 1939 with the establishment of the first Buddha Vihara in New Delhi by the Maha Bodhi Society of India. However, the revival movement got momentum only in 1956 when Dr. B.R. Ambedkar gave a clarion call to his followers to seek refuge in the *Buddha-Dhamma.* Consequently, the Buddhist population in Delhi rose from a meagre figure of 503 in 1951 to 5,466 in 1961; thus registering a striking increase of 98.7 per cent within a short span of five years (1956-61). The Buddhist population in Delhi further rose to 8.720 in 1971. The 1991 Census have shown a substantial increase in the Buddhist population in Delhi. The figure indicated in 1991 Census is 13,906. Thus, Buddhism is taking roots in the Capital.

Buddha *Vihāras*

Prior to 1950, Delhi had only one Buddha *Vihāra.* To-day, there are over twenty five Buddha *Vihāras* catering to the needs of the Buddhist devotees in the Capital. Of these, the important *Vihāras* are : New Delhi Buddha *Vihāra,* Asoka Mission *Vihāra* , Ambedkar Bhavan *Vihāra,* Ladakh Buddha *Vihāra* and Jagajyoti Buddha *Vihāra.*

(I) Buddha *Vihāra* Mandir Marg, New Delhi 110001

The first Buddhist temple to be built in modern times in New Delhi was the Buddha *Vihāra* on Mandir Marg (Reading Road). It was at the instance of Sarbananda Barua, a solitary Buddhist employee in the house-hold of the Viceroy of India, that the Maha Bodhi Society of India approached Government and obtained a piece of land for this *Vihāra.* The foundation stone of the first *Vihāra* in the capital of modern India was laid by K. Yonewaza, Consul General for Japan on 31 October 1936. Raja Seth Jugal Kishore Birla, on being approached by Devapriya Valisinha, General Secretary of the Maha Bodhi Society of India, bore the entire cost of the *Vihāra* and its buildings, and dedicated it to the sweet memory of his father, Raja Baldev Dass Birla. He donated the *Vihāra* to the Maha Bodhi Society of India with the understanding that in the time to come the expenses of upkeep and maintenance will be borne by him, his heirs, executors. The Maha Bodhi Society owes a sense of gratitude to Birlaji for this great munificence. The *Vihāra* was opened by Mahatma Gandhi on

18 March 1939. A replica of the historic Preaching Buddha (Sarnath Museum) is enshrined in the *Vihāra.* The walls have paintings depicting the major events from the life of the Buddha.

The first *Bhikkhu*-in-charge of this *Vihāra* was Ven. Gyanasiri. He was followed by Ven. Mahanama; Ven Dharamadhara; Bhadant D. Shasansiri; Ven Y. Dhammaloka and Ven. Dr. H. Saddhatissa Maha Thera, who later became incharge of the London Buddhist *Vihāra,* London. Ven L. Ariyawansa *Mahā* Thera, who took charge of the *Vihāra* on 7th November, 1950, remained its incharge till his death on 1st October 1994. Presently, Ven. W. Medhananda is the Bhikkhu-in-charge of the Vihara.

With the establishment of this *Vihāra,* Buddhism can be said to have come to the Capital of India. The history of this *Vihāra* is the history of the revival of Buddhism in the Capital. Delhi's first Buddha Jayanti celebrations were held in this *Vihāra* in 1939. Since then the Buddha Jayanti is celebrated here every year.

In 1950, Delhi withnessed the first Buddhist procession which was taken out from this *Vihāra* at the instance of and with the blessings of Baba Saheb Dr. Ambedkar. Since 1951, the Buddha Jayanti celebrations, at the *Vihāra* are being celebrated in a more organised manner. Every year a number of distinguished personalities, eminent scholars and diplomats from the South-East Asian countries participate in this function. The interest shown by National leaders in the activities of this *Vihāra* is more than evident from the list of the participants in the Buddha Purnima Day functions held from 1951 onward. They include : Dr. Kailash Nath Katju, Dr. B.R. Ambedkar, Jawaharlal Nehru, Pandit Govind Ballabh Pant, Morarji Desai, Dr. Rajendra Prasad, Lal Bahadur Shastri, Shrimati Indira Gandhi, Gopal Swarup Pathak and B.D. Jatti.

Apart from the *Buddha Purnima,* thrice Sacred Day, which was declared a public Holiday by Government in 1953 largely through the efforts of Ven. Ariyawansa and others associated with the *Vihāra,* other Buddhist festivals like the *Asadhi Purnima, Aswini Purnima, Maghi Purnima,* etc. are also celebrated at this *Vihāra* in proper style and form. Another important event which is celebrated every year in this *Vihāra* is the birth anniversary of Anagarika Dharmapala, the founder of the Maha Bodhi Society of India. Dharampala was born in Sri Lanka in a Buddhist family on 17 September 1864. He came on pilgrimage to India in 1891. On seeing the sacred Buddhist shrines in ruins and utterly neglected, he was shocked, and decided to devote his remaining life to the cause of Buddhism in India. The Birth Centenary of this pioneer Dhammaduta of modern times was celebrated in 1964-65. In this connection, a number of functions were held at the *Vihāra* premises. The main function was held on 25 October 1964 under the Presidentship of Lal Bahadur Shastri, the Prime Minister of India. It was attended by Mrs. Srimavo Bandaranaika, Prime Minister of Sri Lanka, who, to commemorate the occasion, had brought a Bo-Sapling from the Holy Tree at Anuradhapura for being planted in the Buddha Jayanti Park.

Being close to the Lakshminarayan Temple (Birla Mandir) it is daily visited by thousands of men, women and children of all faiths. It also caters to the needs of the Buddhists from other parts of the world. At this *Vihāra* religious discourses and lectures on Buddhism are delivered from time to time by eminent scholars and religious leaders. It has a small library also.

This *Vihāra* is invariably visited by the distinguished personalities-Presidents, Prime Minsters, Kings-and delegations from the South East Asian Buddhist countries-who visit New Delhi from time to time. Among the Venerable monks from abroad honoured at the *Vihāra,* mention may be made of Ven. M. Ariyawansa Maha Nayaka Thera, Principal of the Pravachanodaya Oriental College, Sri Lanka; H.H. the Dalai Lama; H.H. the Panchen Lama; Rav. Riri Nakayama of Japan; Archbishop Rev. Shodo Okano of Japan; Rev. Kesho Ohtani of

Japan; Ven. Mahasi Sayadow of Burma; the Sangharaja of Thailand; the Sangharaja of Laos; Reverend Y. Sugisaki, Rev. Kyoshim Kawai, Rev. Jonkai Osada and Rev. Shoyu Iwaya-all from Japan; His Holiness Bhamju S. Gambojav Khambo Lama, the Maha Sanghanayaka of Ulanbator, Mangolia; Ven. Dr. Seo Kyung-bo of South Korea, Dr. Kim Kwang-tae of South Korea; Ven Amritananda Maha Thera of Nepal; Ven. Visuddhananda Maha Thera, Sangha Nayaka of Bangladesh.

In view of multifarious achievements, this modest stone-built *Vihāra* can look back with pride on the role played by it in furthering the cause of Buddhism-both at national level and at international level during the last 50 years.

(2) Aśoka Mission *Vihāra*

P.O. Mehrauli, New Delhi-110030

The *Aśoka* Mission *Vihāra,* near Qutab Minar, was established in 1950 by Venerable V. Dhammavara Maha Thera, a Cambodian monk. This *Vihāra* is situated in beautiful, serene and calm environments and caters to the needs of the rural population around. Ven. Lama Lobzang is now the President of Asoka Mission.

(3) Ambedkar Bhavan *Vihāra*

Rani Jhansi Road, New Delhi–110001

The foundation stone of the Ambedkar Bhavan, situated at the interjunction of Rani Jhansi Road and Panchkuan Road, was laid on 15 April 1951 by Babasaheb Dr. B.R. Ambedkar himself. In 1956, one of its rooms was convertsed into a shrine room. This *Vihāra* is managed by the Buddhist Society of India (Bhartiya Baudh Maha Sabha), an organisation founded by Dr. Ambedkar to work for the Buddhist revival in India. The Bhartiya Baudh Maha Sabha organises every year, on the occasion of the Buddha Jayanti, a huge, colourful procession which starts from the historic Red Fort and, after passing through the main bazars in the city, terminates at Ambedkar Bhavan, where a public meeting is held in the evening.

Like Buddha Jayanti, Ambedkar Jayanti, on 14 April, is another major festival for the Indian Buddhists. Of all the functions in Delhi, the function held in the morning on that day in the courtyard of Parliament House is the most impressive. This largely attended function begins with the chanting of sacred Buddhist *suttas* followed by the garlanding of the statue of Dr. Ambedkar, installed on 2 April 1967.

(4) Ladakh Buddha *Vihāra* , Bela Road, Delhi-110054

The Ladakh Buddha *Vihāra,* situated on the bank of river Yamuna, is the most spacious *Vihāra* in Delhi. It has over 40 furnished bed rooms, a meeting hall, a temple and library. This prestigious Institution of the Buddhists of Ladakh was founded by His Holiness Kushak Bakula who is also its President since its inception. It was constructed in 1963 under the kind patronage of Jawaharlal Nehru, the first Prime Minister of India, and was opened by him on 24 February, 1963.

The shrine room of the Ladakh *Vihāra* has three beautiful statues of Lord Buddha, Sāriputta and Moggallana. Six large size paintings, depicting the life of the Buddha, decorate the temple walls.

The Rest House, attached to this *Vihāra,* was constructed by the Government of India at a cost of Rupees 5.50 lakhs for the use of Lamas and other pilgrims from border areas in response to a request made by Ven. Kushak Bakula to the Prime Minister of India. The temple was built with public donations.

In library, the Ladakh Buddha *Vihāra* has a rich collection of ancient Tibetan scriptures. These have been retrieved from the monasteries as well as private sources in Ladakh. The oldest manuscript at the *Vihāra* is 1200 years old. It was written by King Songstsan Gampo of Tibet. The *Vihāra* has also procured all the 16 volumes of the Boom scriptures, which are supplementary to the *Tripitaka,* and are most popular with the adherents of the *Māhayana* Buddhism.

(5) Jagajyoti Buddha *Vihāra*
Sant Nagar, New Delhi-110016

The Jagajyoti Buddha *Vihāra* is just near the newly discovered Rock Edict of Asoka at Bahpur. It was constructed in 1968 by the Bengali Buddhist community in the Capital, at the instance and guidance of Ven. L. Ariyawansa Nayaka Maha Thera.

Twenty other *Vihāras* in the Capital are in : Aśhok Vihār. Budarpur, Baljit Nagar (West Patel Nagar), Bhogal, Dr. Ambedkar Nagar, Govindpuri (main), Govindpuri (DDA Flats), Goverdhan Bihari Colony (Bholanath Nagar), Laxminagar, beyond I.T.O. bridge, (1. established by Ven. Vishudhananda, and 2. Tibetan Temple), Madangiri, Munikra, Pacchim Vihar, R.K Puram, Sector III, Shahdra (I. in Vishwas Nagar, and 2. on Loni Road), Siddharth Colony, Sultanpuri and Japanese Buddhist Temple, D Block, East of Kailash. Most of the Buddha Viharas in Delhi have resident monks. Some of the prominent Buddhist monks in Delhi are ; Ven. Lama Lobzang, Ven. Dhammaviryo, Ven. Vishuddhananda, Ven. Mahanama, Ven. Silanada, Ven. Dr. Satyapal, Ven. Dr. Gyanaratana, Ven. Karunananda, Ven. Satyasheel, Ven. Dr. Doboom Tulku (of Tibet, Ven. Mahaviro (of Thailand), Ven. Vijitadhamma (of Sri Lanka), Ven. W. Medhananda (of Sri Lanka), and Rev. Nakamura (of Japan).

II. Meditation Centres

Delhi now has a permanent Vipassana Meditation Centre. It has been established by the International Vipassana Academy, Igatpuri, Maharshtra, founded by S.N.Goenka. Named as Dhammasota, this centre is situated at Logic Estate Farm, Chhatarpur, Mandir Road, New Delhi-II0030, and contact address is Vipassana Sadhana Sansthan, Hemkunth Towers, 16th floor, 98 Nehru Place, New Delhi - 110019.

There is also a Mahayana Meditation Centre. Its address is Tushita Mahayana Meditation Centre. C 34 A, Nizamudin East, New Delhi - 110013.

III. Buddha Jayanti Park

The Buddha Jayanti Park is a beautiful park on the famous New Delhi Ridge, behind the Buddha Vihara on Mandir Marg. It was laid out in 1956 to commemorate the 2500th Buddha Jayanti Celebrations. Its foundation stone was laid by Prime Minister Jawaharalal Nehru on 23 May 1956. A Bo-sapling brought from the Holy Tree at Anuradhapura in Sri Lanka by Mrs Sirimavo Bandaranaike, the Prime Minister of Sri Lanka was planted in this Park on 25 October 1964 by Lal Bahadur Shastri, the second Prime Minister of India to commemorate the birth centenary of Anagarika Dharmapala, founder of the Maha Bodhi Society of India.

It may be relevant to mention here that Sanghamitta, Asoka's daughter, who like her brother, Mahinda, went as a missionary to Sri Lanka, had taken with her a sapling of the Bodhi Tree under which the Buddha had attained Enlightenment. This Bo-sapling was planted in the Mahamegha garden of Anuradhapura, the capital of Sri Lanka in the third century B. C. Tended with honour and care, through the ages, Anuradhapura Bodhi Tree flourishes to this day, and is one of the most sacred objects of veneration and worship for the Buddhists. Because of this sanctity, the Bodhi Tree in the Buddha Jayanti Park has already become an object of veneration for the Buddhists of Delhi who visit it on the Buddha-Purnima and other sacred days.

IV Buddhist Studies

(1) University of Delhi

The years 1956 marked a milestone in the chequered history of Buddhism. In that year, the Buddhist Era, which commenced on the day of the *Mahā-parinirvāna* of the Buddha, completed, 2,500 years. This historic event was celebrated with great enthusiasm throughout the Buddhist world. To celebrate this great event in a befitting manner in India, the land of the Buddha, a National Committee was appointed by the Government of India under the Chairmanship of Dr. S. Radhakrishnan, Vice-President of India. Other members of the Buddha Jayanti Celebrations Committee were : Chief Ministers of U.P., Bihar and Assam; the Maharaj Kumar of Sikkim; and Ven. Kushak Bakula, the Head Lama of Ladakh. Prime Minister of India was an associate Member.

As was natural, Delhi was chosen as the venue for the Buddha Jayanti functions to be held at national level. The major functions held in the Capital of India were : Laying the foundation stone of the Memorial Monument on the New Delhi Ridge by Jawaharlal Nehru, the Prime Minister of India, on 23rd May 1956; Mass public meeting on 24th May; Opening of the Buddhist Art Exhibition on 3rd November; International Buddhist Symposium on 17-18th November 1956. The programme also envisaged publications - 2,500 Years of Buddhism, Inscriptions of *Aśoka,* a pictorial album; issue of commemorative stamps; and production of a documentary film showing the life of the Buddha in Indian sculpture and paintings.

An important decision taken by the Government of India in 1956 was to establish a Chair for Buddhist Studies at University of Delhi to commemorate the 2,500th Buddha Jayanti Celebrations. An announcement to this effect was made by the President of India, Dr. Rajendra Prasad, at the public meeting held on 24th May 1956 in Ramlila Grounds, Delhi. In pursuance of this decision, Dr P.V. Bapat, an eminent scholar of Buddhism, was appointed as Professor of Buddhist Studies in the University of Delhi. Prof. Bapat joined in February 1957, and the Buddhist Studies were formally inaugurated in October 1957. To begin with, the Buddhist Studies formed part of the Department of Philosophy. Later, in July 1962, an independent Department of Buddhist Studies was created. This Department has now become an important centre of Buddhist Studies.

Apart from teaching Pali the Department of Buddhist Studies offers research facilities to the Post-Graduate students interested in Buddhism. This Department now runs seven courses-Ph. D., M Phil., M. Litt., M.A., and Certificates and Diplomas in *Pāli* and Tibetan languages. Dr. N.H. Samtani was the first scholar to be awarded Ph. D.degree by this Department in 1961. Upto 1987, 50 Ph. D. degrees had been awarded by the Department of Buddhist Studies. And more than 150 students had been awarded M.Phil or M. Litt. degrees by this Department.

The Delhi University library has more than 4,000 volumes which include sets of *Tripitaka* texts in Pali in Roman, Simhalese, Burmese, Siamese and Devanagari Scripts; Chinese Tripitaka; Tibetan *Tripitaka;* full set of *Pāli Attahakathas* in Simhalese script, and so far published in Devanagari script; set of *Suttapitaka* Texts; Sacred Books of the East; Encyclopaedia of Ethics and Religion; and many other important books useful for an in-depth study of Buddhism.

The Department brings out an annual research journal 'Buddhist Studies' which was first published in March 1974. The Department has also brought out 15 other publications so far.

(2) International Academy of Indian Culture

International Academy of Indian Culture, J-22 Haus Khas Enclave, New Delhi-110016, was founded in 1932 by the late Professor Raghuvira. Prof. Dr. Lokesh Chandra, his son, is now Director of the Academy.

The main focus of research by the Academy has been on Indian literature outside her political frontiers, and study of cultural relations with Afghanistan, Central Asia, China, Korea, Japan, Vietnam, Cambodia, Laos, Thailand, Malaysia, Indonesia, Sri Lanka, Burma and other Buddhist countries.

The Academy has so far published Research monographs in the *Suttapitaka Series* number 346 in over 410 hard volumes. They comprise a fascimile edition of 108 volumes of the Mongolian *Tripitaka* entitled "Mongolian Kanjur" in over 80,000 pages; "Sanskrit Texts from the Imperial Palace at

Peking", volumes I-22 comprising a collection of hymns or *dhāranis* recited at the Imperial Palace of Chinese Emperors during the Ch´ing dynasty; "Collected works of Bu-ston", Volumes 1-28 being the works of Bu-ston Rin-chen-grub/ Ratnasiddhi who edited the *Tripitaka; "The Collected Works of Suv-pa-mbhan-po"* in nine volumes; "*Multilingual Buddhist Texts*", volumes 1-12, a collection of Buddhist *Sūtrās* in more than one language, e.g. the *Amitayas-Sūtrās* in Sanskrit, Chinese, Tibetan and Mongolian; Several rare historical chronicles from Tibet have been edited; "*History of Buddhism in Mongolia* by Tsha-hpbel", *Biography of "Chang-lo-tsa-ba Choo-rje-dpal", "Mkhaspahi-dgah-ston"* in four volumes, "*Biography of Atisa and his Disciple Hbromston*".

Recently, the Academy has brought out an English version of Giuseppe Tucci's book, *Mchod-rten-e-tsha-tsha nel Tibet indiano ed occidentale* (Indo-Tibetica I, Rome, 1932) The book titled '*Stupa and tsha-tsha*' has been translated into English for the first time from the original Italian by Uma Vasci and Dr. Lokesh Chandra. This volume is a major contribution to Buddhist art and its significance, its ritual and architecture, as preserved in Tibetan texts and as practised over the centuries. It deals with architectural treatises (like that of *Sahajavilasa*, translated from Sanskrit into Tibetan), the Indian models, the construction techonology of the stupa, its ritual and symbolism. The moulded and other votive stupas recovered from Ladakh, Spiti, Kunuvar and Guge by Prof. Tucci and belonging to the 9-10 centuries have been described.

The Academy also provides research facilities to the interested scholars., who is fact, come from all over the world to make use of its rich, rare and unique library.

V. Museums

(1) National Museum

The National Museum, situated at the crossing of Rajpath and Janpath in New Delhi, was established after Independence in 1949. It has since grown into a premier museum preserving the remains of Indian culture and civilisation of over five thousand years.

The Archaelogical Gallery in the National Museum has four remarkable pieces of sculpture of 2nd century B.C. which once adorned the famous Bharhut stupa in Madhya Pradesh. The first Bharhut exhibit is a Pillar showing *Savanna Karkata Jātāka;* the second is also a pillar showing *Chhadanta Jātāka* on one side and *Mahakapi Jātāka* on the other side. The third Bharhut sculpture is stupa slab; and the fourth is carving of a cave.

Next to Bharhut are three beautiful marble sculptures from Amaravati in Andhra Pradesh dating to the 1st-2nd century A.D. These are : a Stupa Casing slab showing scanes from Buddha's life; Asita's Visit to Suddhodana, the sculpture shows Asita holding the infant Buddha represented by a piece of cloth with footmarks in the palace of Suddhodana; and Buddha in a preaching attitude (symbolic) The Amaravati sculptures are on permanent loan from the British Museum, London. The remarkable limestone sculptures from Nagarjunakonda, Andhra Pradesh, dating to the 2nd-3rd century A.D. are : a frieze depciting scenes from Buddha's life and from the *Jātākas.* The scenes here include Siddhartha immersed in pleasure, *Duta-Jātāka* movie, Sumana brings water from Anotatta lake-Preaching Buddha, the story of the wise lady, *Bhuridata Jātāka,* and the fall of Mandhata; a Stupa slab showing triratnas, three *Purna kumbhas* and lions in row; and yet another Sutpa slab showing *triratnas, purna kumbhas* - Vase of Plenty, stupas, *triratnas* and lions in row.

The Kushana sculptures in stone 2nd century A.D. from Mathura are : Architrave showing Buddha in *dhyāna* and *abhayamudra,* and adoration of the Buddha's turban; another architrave depicting procession of devotees in typical vehicles of the period drawn by bullocks and camels and animals of fancy, like lions with fish tail, and crocodiles with swan's neck, auspicious objects and adoration of the Buddha and Buddha's bowl. The Museum also has a very good collection of *Gandhāra* sculptures and stuccos of 2nd-3rd century A.D. Notable *Gandhāra* schist sculptures include images of the Buddha, Bodhisattvas, Bodhisattva Maitrya, Maya's dream, and Scenes from Buddha's life. The note-worthy *Gandhāra*stuccos include a Bust of Buddha, Heads of Buddha, a meditating Buddha, and a standing Buddha.

The Gupta art collection in the Meseum is represented by a number of beautiful stone images in sitting and standing poses of the Buddha and *Bodhisattvas* from Sarnath-all dating to the 5th-6th centuries A. D. Buddha's life in epitome is also depicted in a 5th century sculpture from Sarnath. The scenes include-*Māya's* dream (the descent of a white elephant into the womb of *Māya* and the Birth of Buddha). The infant Buddha being bathed by *Nāga* Kings, Nanda and Upananda.

The Great Departure; Chandaka receiving the royal robes and ornaments from the Master; The *Bodhisattva* cutting of his hair; Sujata's offering; *Bodhisattva* in conversation with *Nāga* Kalika; and *Bodhisattva's* Meditation. *Māra's* Attack; *Bodhisattva's* Enlightenment; and Buddha's First Sermon. The topmost portion which probably represented Buddha's *Māha-parinirvāna* has broken off. Finally, the National Museum also has a large collection of images of the Buddha, *Bodhisattvas* and Buddhist pantheon of the Pala period, 9-12th centuries A.D. in stone as well as in bronze.

(2) Tibet House Museum

The Tibet House, at 1, Institutional Area, Lodi Road, New Delhi-110003, was established by Holiness the Dalai Lama in 1965 to serve as a centre for the preservation and sustenance of Tibet's Cultural heritage. From its modest beginnings, it has by now grown into a well-organised Cultural Centre of Learning, Art and Religion of the Tibetan People in the Capital of India.

The Tibet House Museum preserves a variety of Tibetan items, as well as ancient and rare objets of art which the people were able to bring with them into Exile. Of these, 53 idols and 45 *Thankas* are displayed as part of the present exhibit in the museum gallery and these are changed from time to time.

In addition to these are the traditional Tibetan ritual objects : jewellery, costumes, household objects, war objects etc. which are on display. There is also a good amount of collected Tibetan stamps, currency notes and coins.

All this collection of rare and ancient objects are of great value to those interested in the study of Tibetan culture and history.

The Tibet House has also a library which contains over 5,000 xylographic prints and about 2,000 photo offset prints of Tibetan manuscripts. a separate English section has recently been created in which books on Tibetology. Buddhology and related subjects are available to the researchers.

The Tibet House also conducts religious discourses from time to time on Buddhist logic, philosophy and meditation by qualified *Dharma* teachers. The Centre also organises annual *Dharma* Discourses conducted by highly accomplished and most revered Tibetan Lamas of all the traditions on the basic and essential subjects of *Mahāyana* Buddhism. The Centre also conducts Tibetan language classes. It has also a Research and Publication Unit.

Ven. Doboom Tulku is presently the Director of the Tibet House, Cultural Centre of H.H. the Dalai Lama.

2. Punjab

The Buddhist revival movement in the Punjab began, as everywhere else in India, towards the close of the 19th century. Anagarika Dharmapala, founder of the Maha Bodhi Society of India, was the first missionary in modern times to bring the message of the Buddha to the people of this ancient land. He visited Kurukshetra, Thanesar, Ludhiana, Amritsar, Lahore, Rawalpindi and Panja Saheb in the months of March-April 1899 and gave a series of lectures on Buddhism.

Following Dharmapala's visit, a few enlightened Punjabis became interested in the teachings of the Buddha and embraced Buddhism. The most notable among them was Rai Bahadur Pandit Sheo Narain, an eminent advocate of Lahore. He not only himself came to the refuge of the Buddha but endeavoured to popularise His teachings as well. With this object in view, Rai Bahadur Sheo Narain wrote three pamphlets in English, namely, Aśoka, Buddhism, and Sarnath Guide. He also wrote a booklet in Urdu. In 1931, when the Mulgandha Kuti *Vihāra,* Sarnath was opened, he gifted all books in his personal library to the Sarnath Library. Rai Bahadur Sheo Narain passed away in 1936. Another notable Punjabi to embrace Buddhism was Dr. Har Dayal, the well-known revolutionary and freedom fighter. Har Dayal was born in Delhi in 1884. After graduating from Delhi, he joined the Punjab University, Lahore. In 1911, he went to the Harvard University in America to study Buddhism but soon he joined the Indian revolutionaries in the States, and eventually planned Ghadar (mutiny) revolt of 1915. Later, in 1927, he joined the School of Oriental and African Studies in London, and was awarded Ph. D. degree by the University of London for his thesis '*The Bodhisattva Doctrine in Sanskrit Literature,* which was published in 1932, and still remains an unsurpassed work in that field. Dr. Har Dayal was prolific writer and wrote some thought-provoking treatises like '*Hints for Self-Culture*'. Har Dayal passed away in 1939.

The most eminent Buddhist produced by modern Punjab is Ven. Dr. Bhadant Anand Kausalyayan. He was born on 5 January 1905 in a Khatri family of village Sohna near Chandigarh. After passing matriculation, Harnamdas, as he was named by his parents, joined the Freedom Movement and suspended education as part of the Non-co-operation Movement. Later, he joined the National College, established by Lala Lajpat Rai at Lahore, and passed B.A., at the age of 19, in 1924. Two years later, his intution prompted him to severe his ties with his kith and kin, and he ventured out into the wilderness of life. While roaming hither and thither in search of inner peace, he per chance met in 1926 Mahapandit Rahul Sankrityayan, who was then known as Swami Ramodardas. Rahulji was at that time an Arya Samajist. Inspired by him, Harnamdas, became a P*arivrajik* and changed his name to Brahmachari Vishvanath. Rahul Sankrityayan also advised him to go round and visit the Buddhist shrines. Thus encouraged, he went round the country from shrine to shrine, getting more and more interested in Buddhism. Towards the end of the year 1927, he received a letter from Rahul Sankrityayan, who had earlier gone to Sri Lanka and was teaching Sanskrit at the Vidyalankara Pririvena, asking him to come to Sri Lanka. On reaching Sri Lanka, Vishvanath immediately started studying *Pāli* and was impressed by the Buddhist doctrine. He was ordained as a Buddhist monk on 10 February 1928 by Venerable L. Dhammananda, Principal of the Vidyalankara Pirivena, Kelaniya and was given the new name of 'Anand Kausalyayan'. About his pilgrimage to Buddhism, Anand Kausalyayan says : "The fact that Buddhism was not a revealed religion was appealing to him, and he found solace in the idea that Buddhist texts were not to be believed un-questioningly. The intellectual freedom of Buddhism and the depth of its social commitment impressed him. He further adds that he had read Har Dayal's advice on choosing an occupation : 'Take the least, give the most to society', and this influenced his decision to become a Buddhist Bhikkhu".[1]

Since 1928 Ven. Anand Kausalyayan, the first Punjabi Buddhist monk of modern times, had devoted all his might to further the cause of Buddhism in India. Bhadant Anand Kausalyayan was a prolific creative Hindi writer. Occasionaly, he also wrote in Punjabi, Urdu and English. His fertile pen has given us more than 40 books on varied subjects. He has also translated Dr. Ambedkar's monumental work *'The Buddha and His Dhamma'* into Hindi as well as in Punjabi. On his return from Sri Lanka, where he was Head of the Hindi Department, Vidyalankara University, Kelaniya from 1959 to 1968, Bhadant

Anand Kausalyayan made Nagpur his permanent abode, and played a major role for about twenty years in sustaining the Buddhist revival movement in Maharashtra. He passed away at Nagpur, at the ripe age of 83 years, on 22 June 1988.

Another eminent Buddhist produced by modern Punjab is Dr. R. L. Soni. He was born in 1904 at Bajwara in Hoshiarpur District. After graduating in Medicine and Surgery in 1929 he visited Burma on a pleasure trip. The Buddhist atmosphere of that country made such an immediate and profound impression on his mind that he settled down for ever in Burma. Six years later, in 1933, he embraced Buddhism. Ever since then Dr. Soni had been devoting all his energies to the cause of the Buddha-*Dhamma.* In 1950, he founded the World Institute of Buddhist Culture. Mandalay, an Institution devoted to the propagation of Buddhism as an instrument of human welfare and world peace. Dr. Soni was an author of distinction, and had written a number of thought-provoking treatises on the Buddhist history, philosophy and culture. Dr. Soni was well-known to Dr. Ambedkar. In December 1954, when Dr. Ambedkar visited Burma, he stayed at Mandalay for about a week as Dr Soni's guest. In fact, the fateful decision of embracing Buddhism in 1956 was taken by Dr. Ambedkar at the residence of Dr. Soni at Mandalay. Dr Soni passed away in Burma on 27 April, 1982.

In the wake of Buddhist renaissance in the Punjab, some Sikh writers were also attracted by Buddhism. The life story of the Buddha so beautifully told by Sir Edwin Arnold in his immortal poem '*The Light of Asia*' was the first to be translated into Punjabi language. A prose translation of '*The Light of Asia*' by Gurbaksh Singh (of Preet Lari) is regarded as a classic in modern Punjabi literature. Prof. Mohan Singh, an eminent Punjabi Poet, translated 'The Light of Aisa' into poetry. First Published in 1944, this poetic 'Asia da Channan' remains to this date the most popular book on Buddha's life in Punjabi language. A part of *Dhammapada,* the most popular Buddhist text, was first of all translated into Punjabi by S. Kapoor Singh,

ICS. The Buddhist studies in Punjab received impetus when Dr. Lal Mani Joshi, a distinguished Buddhist scholar, joined in 1968 the Department of Religious Studies in Punjabi University, Patiala as Associate Professor in Buddhist Studies and became Professor and Head of the Department of Religious Studies as well as the Dean of Faculty of Religious Studies, Punjabi University, Patiala (1980-81). Prof. Joshi translated *Dhammapada* into Punjabi and also added *Pāli* text in Gurmukhi script. This was published by the Punjabi University in 1969.

The first Sikh Scholar to obtain Degree of Doctor in Philosophy in Buddhism is Dr. Harcharan Singh Sobti, M.A.L.L.B. Ph.D. Dr. H.S.Sobti was born in 1937 at Dhamial, District Rawal Pindi, now in Pakistan. He migrated to Delhi in 1947 after the Partition. Dr. Sobti pursued interdisciplinary studies in a regular way. He was awarded Degree of Doctor of Philosophy in Buddhist Studies for his doctoral thesis, '*Nibbāna in Early Buddhism* (based on *Pāli* sources from 6th B.C to 5th A.D.) by the University of Delhi in 1983. He published his Doctoral thesis in 1985 and *Studies in Buddhism and Sikhism* in 1986. He has also edited. E. Obermiller's *Nirvāna in Tibetan Buddhism* (1987) *Prajña pāramitā* in *Tibetan Buddhism* (1988), and *Vipassana : The Buddhist Way* (1992).

Statistically speaking, the modern State of Punjab does not have many Buddhists. In fact, there were practically no Buddhists in this State till 1956 when the Buddhist revival movement in India entered into an era of intense activity following the lead given by the late Dr. B.R. Ambedkar. Therefore, almost all the Buddhists in Punjab are new converts. In 1961, the population of Buddhists in Punjab was 1200 only. Twenty years later, the 1961 Census showed the population of Buddhists in Punjab (799) and Chandigarh (454). So the position remained more or less the same. However, the position has now considerably changed for the better. According to 1991 Census. the Buddhist population in the Punjab has risen from 799 to 24,930; thus indicating a whopping rise of 3020 per cent during the 1981-1991 decade.

Out of 24,930 Buddhists, 16,627 live in rural areas, and 8,303 in urban areas. The largest Buddhist population is in the Jalandhar and Hoshiarpur districts.

In the early stages, the neo-Buddhist movement in Jalandhar was spearheaded by L.R. Balley, the eidtor and publisher of Bheem Patrika, a fortnightly journal in Hindi/Punjabi founded by him in 1958. However, the Buddhist movement in Jalandhar took concrete shape only in 1980 when the organisers of Dr. B.R. Ambedkar Study Circule, founded in 1976 purchased a plot of land at a cost of Rs. 20,000/- in the new colony of Siddharth Nagar, on Nakodar Road, and handed it over to the newly formed Buddhist Society of India (Punjab Branch) for constructing a Buddha Vihara. The first major step taken by the Buddhist Society of India was to organise a mass conversion ceremony at the site of the Buddha Vihara on 14 October 1981 where a large number of people embraced Buddhism. The Buddhist Society of India (Punjab), the chief functionaries of which are : Kartar Chand, Sagli Ram, Hussan Lal Baudh and Ram Lal, has since built the first Buddha Vihara in Jalandhar city. The Siddharth Nagar Buddha Vihara has by now become an active centre of religious and cultural activities in Jalandhar, and has a resident monk also.

One of the greatest promoters of Buddhism in modern Punjab is Mahashya Krishna Kumar Bodhi of Nawan Shehar Doaba, a Tehsil town in district Jalandhar. Born in 1921 in a Khatri family of Nawan Shehar, Krishan Kumar Bodhi is now a leading businessman in that town. For over two decades he was an active member of the Arya Samaj, and supporter of the cause. Not happy with the caste inequalities in the society, Krishan Kumar was attracted by the radical views of Babasaheb Dr. Ambedkar in this regard which came to his notice through the writings of Sant Ram, B.A. (1886-1989) in 'Kranti', a monthly organ of the Jat-Pat Todak Mandal. Later, on reading Dr. Ambedkar's monumental work, 'The Buddha and His Dhamma' he was so much fascinated by the Dhamma that

Krishan Kumar immediately decided to adopt the Buddhist way of life. Accordingly, he embraced Buddhism in 1963, and adopted 'Bodhi' as surname. Ever since then, he has proved to be a great benefactor of Buddhism in the Punjab.

Krishan Kumar Bodhi founded in 1980 the Punjab Buddha Mahasabha, and initiated a series of steps to popularise Buddhism. In order to give impetus to the Buddhist movement, the Punjab Buddha Mahasabha, under his leadership organised mass conversion ceremony at Hoshiarpur on 10 March 1991 where over 3000 persons hailing from Hoshiarpur, Phagwara, Jalandhar, Nawan Shehar, Nakodar, Phillaur, Ropar, Muketsar, Faridkot and Sangrur (Longowal) embraced Buddhism The deeksha vows to the new initiates at this historic ceremony were administered by Ven. Dr. Satya Pal, Reader in the Department of Buddhist studies, University of Delhi. Since, 1987, the Punjab Buddha Mahasabha is also bringing out a monthly journal 'Baudh Dharma Prachark', of which the publisher as well as primary financial supporter is Krishan Kumar Bodhi.

Another good acquisition of Buddhism in Punjab is Dr. Surendra Ajnat, M.A. (Hindi & Sanskrit), Ph. D. (US.A. & India) of Banga, district Jalandhar. He is now working as Head of the Department of Hindi in the B.A.M. Khalsa college, Garh Shankar, district Hoshiarpur. Dr. Ajnat was born in an orthodox Brahmin family of village Moron, Tehsil Phillaur, district Jalandhar on 12 August, 1947. Rebel by nature, Dr. Ajnat came to Buddhism inspired by the life and teachings of Dr B.R. Ambedkar. Having been fully convinced of the utility of the Buddha-Dhamma for the welfare of mankind, Dr. Surendra Ajnat is making a conscious effort to popularise Buddhism. Besides delivering innumerable lectures at Conferences and Study Camps, he has by now published scores of articles and pamphlets on various aspects of Buddhism and Ambedkarism-mostly in Hindi and Punjabi.

The author of this work has also contributed a bit to the Buddhist movement in Punjab through his writings. I (D.C.

Ahir) was born on 20 February 1928 at village Bath Klan, Tehsil Nakodar, District Jalandhar. After serving the Government of India for more than 40 years, I retired from service on 28 February 1986 as Director from the Ministery of Surface Transport, New Delhi.

I became interested in Buddhism in 1950, and soon became a frequent visitor to the New Delhi Buddha Vihara. In 1956, I was lucky to be associated with the 2500th Buddha Jayanti celebrations in my official capacity as Assistant Director (Publicity) in the Department of Tourism, Government of India. The vast literature on Buddhism which passed through my hands at that time forcefully stimulated my interest in Buddhism, and when Babasaheb Dr. B.R.Ambedkar, whom I had last met on 8 October 1956 at 26 Alipur Road, embraced Buddhism, I followed suit; my Dhamma Gurus being Bhadant Anand Kausalyayan and Ven. Ariyawansa. In order to formalise this change of religion, I submitted a declaration to my Department on Ist October 1960 to the effect that "I have since embraced Buddhism and that necessary changes be made in official records". So all my subsequent promotions as Under Secretary (1972), Deputy Secretary (1978) and Director (1986) were as a Buddhist.

I began writing on Buddhism in 1960. And by the time I retired in February 1986, I had published a number of well-researched treatises on Buddhism. After retirement, I have been devoting more and more of my time to literary pursuit, and the result has been rewarding. By now, I have published more than 25 books on Buddhism and Ambedkarism. Some of the important books published since 1986 are : *Buddhist Shrines in India; Heritage of Buddhism; Buddhism in North India; The Pioneers of Buddhist Revival in India; Buddhism in Modern India; Buddhism in South India; Himalayan Buddhism : Past and Present; Buddha Gaya Through The Ages; Asoka The Great; A Panorama of Indian Buddhism; The Status of Laity In Buddhism; The Legacy of Dr. Ambedkar; Dr. Ambedkar And Punjab; Dr. Ambedkar, Buddhism and Social Change (Co-edited); Buddhist Revolution And Counter-*

Revolution In Ancient India; Dr. Ambedkar's Vision of Dhamma : An Assessment.

Two of my books have also been translated and published in Punjabi. These are : 'Buddhism and Ambedkar' published in Punjabi in 1983 by Dr B.R. Ambedkar Study Circle. Jalandhar, and 'Buddhism in the Punjab, Haryana and Himachal Pradesh' published in Punjabi in 1991 by Dr. Ambedkar Mission Society, Bedford, England.

The first Buddha Vihara to be built in Hoshiarpur district is at Anandgarh (Mehlanwali) village near Hoshiarpur. Established by the Punjab Buddha Maha Sabha, the Anandgarh Vihara has come up as a result of the generosity of a Sidhu family, one of whose member, Gurmukh Sidhu, lives in England. The foundation stone of this Vihara was laid by Bhadant Anand Kausalyayan on 14 April 1983 on a spacious plot of land donated by the Sidhu family. A beautiful Buddha image was installed in this Vihara on the Buddha Jayanti day in 1984 by the late Sohan Lal Shastri, the vetern Ambedkarite scholar. The Anandgarh Buddha Vihara is being looked after by Ramesh Sidhu.

This Vihara was named 'Ananda Vihara' after the name of Bhadant Anand Kausalyayan. But the name also represents the village Anand Garh. It also indicates the state of happiness (anand), and the good thing is that plans are afoot to establish a Vipassana (Buddhist Meditation) Centre in the vicinity of this Vihara on a 6 acre plot donated by a Vipassana meditator. Modalities for establishing the first Vipassana Centre in Punjab are being worked out by Gurmukh Sidhu, a Vipassana Assistant Teacher, in consultation, with S. N. Geenka, the foremost exponent of Vipassana in India, and founder of the Vipassana International Academy, Igatpuri (Maharastra). The Vipassana Centre, when established in Punjab will be known as 'Dhamma Dhwaja'.

The Buddhist movement is once again gaining momentum in Punjab as a result of the efforts of the Baudh Dharma Prachar Samiti founded in 1996 by S.L.Gindha, Tarsem Lal

Chahl and some other Punjabi Buddhists living in England. In August 1996, the Samiti launched special Dhamma-Diksha drive in Jalandhar district, and converted hundreds of dalits to Buddhism. Encouraged by the response, the Samiti has decided to construct Buddha Viharas at Jalandhar, Hoshiarpur, Nawan Shehar Doaba, Nakodar, Phillaur and Ludhiana in order to cater to the needs of the neo-Buddhists, and to disseminate the message of the Buddha among the masses. Another Buddha Vihara, named as 'Saddhatissa Buddha Vihara' has been established by B.R.Sampla of England at his native village, Sofi Pind, near Jalandhar. Yet another good news is that Advocate S.L. Virdi, who embraced, Buddhism in 1991, is planning to make Phagwara an active centre of Buddhism. Thus Buddhism is making steady progress in Punjab.

3. Chandigarh

Now we come to Chandigarh, presently the twin capital of Punjab and Haryana pending final decision regarding its transfer to Punjab. The moving spirit behind the Buddhist movement in the Union Territory of Chandigarh is Ch. Shiv Dev Sigh (formerly Shiv Ram Sabar). While working at Simla, he became interested in Buddhism, and embraced Buddhism in 1968 at the New Delhi Buddha Vihara from the Ven. L. Ariyawansa Maha Thera. He came to Chandigarh in 1972 with the transfer of his office (A.G.Punjab) from Simla to Chandigarh. In 1976, in association with some Barua Buddhists, he founded the Chandigarh Buddhist Association. And with the help of its members and some Thai students studying in Chandigarh, the Association purchased in 1977 a plot measuring two kanals just outside the red line of village Khuda Ali Sher, a distance of 5 kilometres from Chandigarh, at a cost of Rs. 21,776. The acquired land is ideally situated at the foot of a hillock. The Chandigarh Association has since built there two big rooms, one rain-shelter, and a small shrine room where a Bronze Image of the Buddha has also been installed in the Asoka Buddha Vihara. Besides providing more facilities in this complex, the Chandigarh Association is also planning to construct a Buddha Vihara in Chandigarh Proper at a suitable site for which efforts are on.

That the efforts of Chandigarh Buddhist Association are bearing fruit is evident from the fact that the Buddhist population in Chandigarh has gone up from 454 in 1981 to 799 in 1991, *i.e*, an increase of 54% in the 1981-1991 decade.

The Chandigarh Museum, known as the Government Museum and Art Gallery, in sector 10–C, provides a link with the glorious past of Buddhism in the North-Western region. The largest number of exhibits in the Chandigarh Museum are of the Gandhara School of art. These came as part of its 40 per cent share of the objects from the Lahore Museum. The Museum has more than 150 Gandhara scuptures of the Kushana period discovered from various Buddhist sites, especially Taxila and other Buddhist sites (now in Pakistan).The Gandhara sculptures in Chandigarh Museum include images of the Buddha (in various postures), Bodhisattvas and Scenes from Buddha's life. The Museum has also a number of Terracotta and Stucco Heads of the Buddha and Bodhisattvas.

4. Haryana

The pace of Buddhist movement in Haryana has been rather slow. In 1961, the state of Haryana had 746 Buddhists. And 20 years later, in 1981, this figure stood at 761: thus showing practially no progress. However, the Buddhist movement is now gaining momentum in Haryana as the 1991 Census have revealed an enormous increase in the Buddhist population. As against 761 in 1981, Haryana had 2058 Buddhists in 1991. This shows an increase of 170.43% during the 1981-1991 decade. Of these 2058 Buddhists in Haryana, 529 live in rural areas and the rest 1529 in urban areas. In spite of this, however, no Buddha Vihara has so far been built in Haryana.

5. Himachal Pradesh

We now turn to Himachal Pradesh where Buddhism has survived through the ages. In 1961, Himachal Pradesh had 19,220 Buddhists. In 1971, there were 35,937 Buddhists in this state. And in 1981, Himachal Pradesh had 52,629 Buddhists. According to 1991 Census, the population of Buddhists in Himachal Pradesh is 64,081. Out of them, 54,020 live in rural areas, and the rest 10,061 in urban areas. The largest concentration of Buddhist population in Himachal Pradesh is in the Lahul and Spiti valleys. In 1971, this district had 61.53% Buddhist population. Next comes Kinnaur district with 14.22% Buddhist population. Let us now see to what extent the Himalayan Buddhists are practising their religion.

The valleys of Lahul and Spiti lie at a height of 10000 to 16000 above sea level and are separated from the Kulu valley in Himachal Pradesh by the famous Rohtang Pass, which is also known as the Pass of the Dead. The Lahul valley lies beyond the Rohtang Pass towards the north comprising the watersheds of the Chandra and the Bhaga rivers which later on join to form the Chenab. In area, it is 22000 sq. miles and has an average altitude of 12000 ft. Spiti, which lies to the east of Kulu in the extreme north east corner, beyond the Rohtang Pass, in 2,931 sq. miles in area. Spiti, locally pronounced Piti, is a Tibetan word meaning middle province. It is bounded on three sides by Ladakh, Tibet and Bushahr (Rampur). The valley of Kinnaur lies on both the banks of river Sutlej around its uppermost region bordering Tibet.

Buddhism is said to have entered Lahul and Spiti sometime in the early centuries of the Christian Era even though it was introduced into the country of Himalayas in the third century B.C. by the missionaries led by Ven. Majjhima who were deputed by *Aśoka* to convert the people of the Himalayan region as a part of his *Dhamma-Vijaya* campaign. Their bonds with Buddhism became stronger when the famous Padmasambhava sojourned in these valleys on his way to Tibet in 747-48 A.D. One of the greatest preachers of Buddhism in this area was Rin-chen-bzang-po (Ratnabhadra, 958-1055 A.D.) who is said to have been born at Sumra in Kinnaur. The ancient monasteries in this region go back to the 11th century and are believed to have been founded by him.

The Buddhists of Lahul, Spiti and Kinnaur follow the Tibetan form of Buddhism, and their monks are called Lamas. Owing to proximity to Tibet, the impact of the Tibetan culture on the people of this region is quite significant and is visible in many ways. Their temples, gompas, monasteries have Tibetan names. The main shrine in each monastery is called Lha-khang, and images of the Buddha, *Bodhisattvas* and other divinities are installed there. Each monastery has also a hall for teaching purposes. It is called *Dukhang,* the assembly hall. Some of the monasteries have beautiful paintings depicting scenes from the *Jātakas* and the life of the Buddha. At the entrance to every village, there is always a chorten, a replica of ancient stupa. The erection of these chortens is considered an act of piety; hence their number is large and they can be seen every where. In Kinnaur as well as in Lahul and Spiti, the famous *Mahāyāna* mantra '*Om Mani Padme Hum*' (Hail thou possessor of Jewel Lotus) is considered by the Buddhists as saviour from all dangers, and is almost continuously recited by the devout persons. Not only that, it is often written on a piece of cloth or inscribed in Tibetan script on a stone and left on the spot where it is pronouned by the devotee. Such monuments are called m*ani* walls and can be seen every where near villages, on tops of passes, near fordes and on the banks of rivers.

At present, there are about 30 monasteries each in Lahul, Spiti and Kinnaur. The important monasteries in Lahul are at Kyelang, Kardang, Gurmrang, Gemur, Jholing, Shashin and Tupchilling; in Spiti the important monasteries are at Dhankar, Gungri, Hansa, Ki Kibar, Losar and Tabo and in Kinnaur they are at Chini, Kanum, Lipa, Nako and Poo. Apart from the monasteries, many families have a chapel of their own.

As in Tibet, the Lamas of Himachal Pradesh are also

divided into four main sects. The oldest sect is the *Nying-ma-pa* which is directly based on the teachings of Padmasambhava who introduced Buddhism in Tibet in the eighth century A.D., and is called Guru Rimpoche by the Tibetans. The *Kar-gyu-pa* sect or School of Oral Tradition is said to have been founded in AD 1050, by the Tibetan Lama Marpa, a friend of Atisa (Dipankara Srijnana), and disciple of the Indian Tantrist, Naropa, Head of the Nalanda University in Bihar in the 11th century. Another great exponent of this sect was Mila-ra-pa, the famous poet-saint of Tibet. These sects are also known as 'Red Hat' sects. The third sect Sakya-pa or Saskya-pa derives its name from the colour of the soil where their first monastery was located in Tibet. Founded in A.D. 1071, this sect became poweful in the 13th century, but later declined. The fourth sect, called the Ge-lug-pa (School of the Virtuous) or 'Yellow Hat' sect is the reformed sect founded by the saint Tson-kha-pa around 1400 AD. His Holiness the Dalai Lama belongs to this sect. In Himachal Pradesh, the Kargyupa and the Gelugpa sects are the most popular sects. The sect-wise distribution of monasteries in Lahul, Spiti and Kinnaur is somewhat as under :[4]

Kargyupa-Dug-pa 40 (28 in Lahul and 12 in Kinnaur; Gelugpa 37 (I in Lahul, 21 in Spiti and 15 in Kinnaur); Nyingmapa 12 (7 in Spiti and 5 in Kinnaur); and Sakyapa 2 (in Spiti).

Kyelang, the district head quarters of Lahul, has an impressive Buddhist monastery. The Shashur gompa, here is said to have been founded by Lama Dewa Gyastasho of Ladakh in the 17th Century AD.

The most important monastery in Lahul is the Guru Ghantal monastery at Tupchilling. It is said to be located on the site where Guru Padmasambhava meditated before going to Tibet in A.D. 747. Initially this monastery was called Guru Gandhola. The world Gandhola in Tibetan means the Untainted (pure) House and refers to the holy site of Buddha's enlightenment at Both Gaya. This monastery believed to be the site of Padmasambhava's enlightenment came to be known as Guru Gandhola. In course of time, this was distorted by the foreigners and the monastery came to be known as Guru Ghantal. The monastery has a wooden image of the Buddha which is said to have been installed in th 11th century A. D. by Lama Rin-chen-bzang-po of Kinnaur.

The Tabo monastery known as the Chos-hkor, is the largest monastery in Spiti. It has as many as nine temples. Of these, atleast five temples are traced back to the 11th century A.D. Three most important temples are; the Golden Temple, the Large Temple of Drompton, and the Temple of Enlightened Gods. The Golden Temple has beautiful murals of the divinities and the protective deities on the walls. The ceiling of the temple is painted with Gandharvas, birds and flora motifs. The Large Temple of Drompton has a large painted figure of the Buddha flanked by Sāriputta on the right and Mahā Moggallana on the left. The side walls have figures of the Eight Medicine Buddhas. The Temple of Enlightened Gods has the largest number of images.

The Tabo Monastery, also known as the Himalayan Ajanta, completed 1,000 years of its existence in 1996. The 1000th Years Celebrations of the Tabo Monastery were organised by the Government of Himachal Pradesh for two weeks from 20 June 1996 onward, and attracted a large number of pilgrims from the Buddhist countries.

Another important monastery in Spiti is at Ki. The walls of the assembly hall (du-khang) of this monastery have beautiful murals. Yet another important monastery in this valley is the Pin monastery at Gungri which is believed to have been founded by Padmasambhava in the 8th century A.D.

Of all the Buddhist temples in Himachal Pradesh, those at Kanum, a tiny village in Kinnaur are most important on account of their architecture wall paintings and literary treasures. Situated in the lap of hills at an elevation of 9600 ft, Kanum is about 186 miles from Shimla, the capital of Himachal

Pradesh, and 33 miles beyond Kalpa, the district head quarters of Kinnaur. The Tehsil headquarters, Poo, is 16 miles farther away. The Hindustan-Tibet Road, a National Highway, passes about 2 miles down the village along the right bank of the river Sutlej.

Kanum is one of the oldest villages in Kinnaur. About its name it is said that long long ago, while ploughing the barren land in the village, the head of the family of Lactas found a beautiful stone inscribed with '*Ka*' in Tibetan language. He brought this stone home, and after some time consulted a Lama from Tibet. The Lama told him that '*ka*' in Tibetan scripture means ' the divine command; it being the first letter of *Kangyur.* Thus the village came to be known as Kanum, a place of sacred books.

Kanum is a wholly Buddhist village. It has as many as seven monasteries. These are.[5]

Kangyur : The Kangyur monastery, the most ancient in Kanum, is situated in the heart of the village. Its two storey building houses a very fine library which contains 108 volumes of *Kangyur (Kanjur)* and 225, volumes of *Tangyur (Tanjur)* books written in Tibetan script; a rare collection indeed for a village library. According to Rahul Sankrityayan, the wooden stencils of these books were engraved in Northang monastery in Central Tibet in the 16th Century.

The famous Hungarian-born Tibetan scholar, Alexander Csoma de Koros (1784-1842) had made use of this library in compiling his *Tibetan English Dictionary.* He stayed at Kanum for over three years in 1827-30; collected and arranged 40,000 Tibetan words and nearly completed the *Tibetan English Dictionary,* which was later published by the Asiatic Society of Bengal, Calcutta.

Lundup Ganfel Gompa : This is the biggest monastery in Kanum and is situated on the top of the village. This monastery is also called *Kache-lha-Khanq,* i.e. the Kashmiri temple, by the local people. According to Rahul Sankrityayan, it was built by

Maha Pandit Shakya Virbhadra[6] of Kashmir, the last Sangharaja of India, who ran from India in about A.D. 1213 and lived for 10 years in Tibet. On his way back to his birth place in Kashmir, he stayed at Kanum and got constructed a *Vihāra*. Shakya Virbhadra in Bhot is known as '*Khache-Pan-Chhen*' (Kashmiri Pandit). Hence the *Vihāra* constructed by him came to be known as *Khache-lha-Khang*. The present monastery was built on the site of the old temple by Lama Tomo Geshe who lived in Kinnaur about 100 years ago.

This *Gompa* has on its walls the nicest and beautiful mural paintings depicting various phases of the life of the Buddha. The monastery has also good collection of religious books and Buddha statues made of clay, and sandalwood.

Lachao Labrang or Lha-khang Locahlama : This monastery commemorates the visit of the Rimpoche Locha Lama of Tashilhunpo, Tibet who visited Kanum in A.D. 1897 when he came to consecrate the Buddhist temple built at Rampur by Tikka Raghunath Singh of Bushahr.

Tasi Choeling : It is a Nunnery where Buddhist nuns called Jomos reside. Besides the prayer hall, nunnery provides accommodation for as many as 25 Jomos.

The remaining three shrines at Kanum are : *Surpu Gompa, Namgyal Chorten,* and the temple of the village deity, *Dabla devata.*

Another important monastery in Kinnaur is at Kano village. This monastic complex of four large temples is called 'the Lotsaba Lha-khang' after its founder, Richen-bzng-po, who was a great Buddhist revivalist in this region in the 11th century A.D.

After Kinnaur, we come to the Kulu-Kangra valley. The important Buddhist centres in this valley are Kulu and Dharmsala. The main transit railhead for both of them is Pathankot. The town of Kulu, which is about 175 miles beyond Pathankot, has even in the past played an important role in the history of Buddhism in the Punjab. In the 7th century A.D. it was such an important centre of Buddhism that Hiuen Tsang; not minding the dangerous route through the high mountain passes and deep ravines, came all the way from Jalandhar to Kulu. At that time, it was known as Kuluta and had as many as 20 *Sangharamas*. Kulu is now the headquarters of the Himalayan Buddhist Society which was established by the local Buddhists in 1942 in order to give impetus to the renaissance movement amongst the Buddhists of this valley. There is also a Himalayan Buddhist Cultural Association at Manali. A Tibetan Buddhist temple has also come up at Manali.

Dharmsala, the headquarters of Kangra district, has a beautiful newly built *Gelugpa Tibetan monastery*. Being the permanent abode of His Holiness the Dalai Lama, who took aslyam in India in 1959 under compelling circumstances, Dharmsala has now become a place of pilgrimage for the Buddhists. The Council of Religious Affairs of His Holiness the Dalai Lama which manages Tibetan institutions in India has also its hedquarters at Dharmsala.

In Kangra district, a large Buddhist monastic complex has recently come up at Bir, a village in Tehsil Palampur. Built by the Tibetan settlers, the complex has five monasteries. These monasteries have gaint images of the Buddha, Padmasambhava, and other divinities. One of these monasteries, known as Sherab-ling, or "the land of wisdom", is located on a hill top with forests all around. The main temple, a three-story building, faces a courtyard enclosed by classrooms and living cells for monks. The ornately carved throne of the Tai Situ, decorated with the traditional *dharmachakra* and dragons dominate the shrine room. Sherab-ling is a vast project designed to cater to the spiritual, cultural, medical, and educational needs of the people. The Complex has furnished guest houses and retreat houses with meditation cells. Adequate educational facilities have also been provided. Bir is now attracting many visitors, from India and abroad, who come here for study and meditation.

Another Buddhist monastery in district Kangra is at

Tilokpur, 20 miles below Dharmsala, and one the straight way from Pathankot to Mandi. It is a *Mahāyāna* Monastery for Nuns.

Rewalsar, 20 km from Mandi, is the most important Buddhist shrine in Mandi district. Here, a fair called Sichu takes place every year in the month of *Phalguna* (March-April) in the Mani-pani temple-an old shrine dedicated to Guru Padmasambhava who meditated here in A.D. 747 before going to Tibet. Since Padmasambhava, also known as Guru Rimpoche, was the first propagator of Buddhism in Tibet and is revered by all the followers of Lamaism, irrespective of sects, this fair is attended by a considerable number of Buddhists from all over Himachal Pradesh, and even Ladakh.

There is only one ancient Buddhist temple in Shimla district. It is at Rampur and was built by Tikka Raghunath Singh of Bushahr in 1897. Recently, a large Tibetan monastery has been established at Sanjauli, near Shimla, the capital of Himachal Pradesh. Yet another Tibetan monastery has been built at Kusampati, near Shimla. This monastery is said to be a replica of the famous monastery at Dorjidak in South Lhasa, Tibet, which was ndestroyed by the Chinese in 1949. The newly built monastery was opened by His Holiness The XIV Dalai Lama on Ist August 1992.

An effort to revive Buddhism in the districts of Bilaspur, Mandi and Shimla is being made by Professor Narain Chand Parashar, a Buddhist, Ex-Member of Parliament and presently Minister of Education and Culture in the Government of Himachal Pradesh. Under the aeigs of Shri Siddharth Saddharam Sangham, a Society established by him with headquarters at Shimla, the message of the Buddha is being disseminated among the masses. Prof Parashar is also a good speaker and writer, and has translated Dhammapada into Pahari language for the benefit of the people of the State.

References

1. Anand, Kausalayayan, *Bhikkshu Ke Patter* (Hindi) (1940)
2. *Census of India 1961,* paper No. 1 of 1963-Religion.
3. *Census of India 1981,* Series-I, India, Paper 3 of 1984, Household population by Religion of Head of Household, pp xii and xvi.
4. O.C.Handa, *Buddhist Monasteries in Himachal Pradesh,* pp. 185-92.
5. *Census of India 1961,* Volume XX-Part VI-No. 12 Himachal Pradesh- A Village Survey of Kanum.
6. Rahul Sankrityayan, *Kinner Desh* (Hindi)

Chapter X

The Influence of Buddhism on Sikhism

In this chapter, we turn to the influence of Buddhism on Sikhism, the predominent religion of modern Punjab.

Sikhism is younger to Buddhism, by over 2000 years as *Gurū Nānak,* its founder, was born in 1469 A.D. whereas Lord Buddha lived in the 6th century B.C. Inspite of that, and the fact the that Sikhism arose at a time when almost all traces of Buddhism had disappeared from India, the religion of the Buddha can be said to have left its mark on the Sikh religion. To quote only a few instances:

In the *Ādi-Granth,* the holy book of the Sikhs, there is a reference to Lord Buddha at more than one place, though sometimes He is grouped with the *Siddhas* and *Yogis* for praising and eulogising God as in the following hymns:

1. *Sivas* speak of Him, *Siddhas* speak of Him, The *Buddhas* He has created, proclaim Him.[1]

2. On the top of them, How many adepts, *Buddhas* and Yogis are there. His worshippers are numberless, saith Nanak.[2]

The Buddha did not recommend the worship of God and a Buddhist does not bother about Him. The Sikhs, however, lean heavily on God. Sikhism, therefore, like all other theistic religions differs in theory from Buddhism. But the influence of Buddhism on its practical aspects is visible in many ways. Mark what Sher Singh says in *'Philosophy of Sikhism'* regarding the influence of the Buddha and Buddhism on the Sikh religion. "From other Hindu systems Sikhism does not so much differ in theory as in practice, but in the case of

Buddhism, the opposite is true. There is no borrowing in theory but the influence is visible in some practical aspects. Buddha tried to abolish caste and his idea of brotherhood becomes an important theme with Nanak. Purity of heart and sincerety in our dealings with mankind were the essence of religion for Nānak. These virtues were the first to be emphasized by Buddha. No sanctity of any particular language is the third common element in the teachings of the two prophets. Buddha preached in the spoken language of the people and was the first Indian prophet to become a missionary. In these respects Nānak very closely resembles Buddha."[3]

When the Buddha traversed and sanctified the soil of India, the self indulgent people lived the lives of luxury and sin, and the ascetics practised self-mortification in various ways. The Buddha declared both these ways as futile and unworthy of attaining *Nirvāna*. He preached the Middle Path that is avoidance of the two extremes-the life of luxury and passion and the life of self-torture through penance. The founder of Sikhism preached the essence of the Middle Path in another sense. He exhorted his disciples to avoid the extremes of Hinduism and Islam, the two religions prevalent in the Punjab in those days. Lord Buddha denied the authority and sanctity of the Vedas, denounced the caste system, sacrifices and rituals, and exhorted His followers to lead a simple and moral life. He emphasized the need of self-less service to the humanity and gave the clarion call of *Bahujana Hitaye, Bahujana Hitāye* (welfare and well-being of the many). The Sikh Gurus almost preached literally these Buddhistic ideas. In the *Rahtnāmā* or Book of Guidance, *Gurū* Gobind Singh, the tenth and last Guru, exhorts the Sikhs not to follow the doctrines of the Vedas, Puranas and Quran. He further tells them not to perform *Shradhas* or ceremonies of the anniversaries of the dead. Regarding caste, the Guru says, 'there must be no caste and all must be equal, no man is greater than the other'. The ideal of service is also equally emphasized in Sikhism.

The *Buddha,* the *Dhamma* and the *Sangha,* commonly known as Triple Gem *(Tri-Ratna)* are the three basic principles of Buddhism. When the Buddhists take the Triple Refuge (Tri-Sarana) it means that they take refuge in the Buddha (Founder, Teacher or Guru), His Word, and the Assembly of the venerable monks (both past and present). Almost the same idea of *Tri-Sarana* is reflected in the Sikh formula of having faith in the Guru, the Word and the Sangat. The only difference in the Triplegem of the Sikhs is that the Bhikkhu *Sangha* is replaced here by the congregration of the lay devotees but the pattern remains the same.[4]

Every lay Buddhist is expected to lead his life in accordance with the Five Precepts *(Panch Sheel)* enunciated by the Buddha. These precepts are vows to abstain from killing, stealing, debauchery, telling lies and taking intoxicating drinks and drugs. These precepts are, therefore, necessary ingredient of a Buddhist's daily life. The Sikhs too have vows to take, but in their case these are external signs of body. The Sikhs are enjoined to wear the five K's, *viz,* the *Kesh (long hair), Kachhā* (short breeches), the *Karā* (ironbangle), the *Kirpān* (sword) and the *Kanghā* (comb). Though the five Precepts and the five K's differ from each other, the fact remains that the' five vows' are important in both the religions. The figure of five is dear to the Buddhists and the Sikhs alike for another reason also. Lord Buddha delivered His First Sermon at Sarnath before five recluses, *Bhikkhūs.* The last Guru of the Sikhs too, first of all, initiated five Sikhs, known as the 'Five Beloved' *(Panj Piyare)* when he transformed the peaceful followers of Nanak into a militant class and gave them the name of *Khālsa.*

The four Noble Truths expounded by the Buddha lay emphasis on suffering *(Dukkha).* He says, 'Birth is suffering, decrepitude is suffering, so are sickness and death suffering'. The all-pervading force of suffering is also accepted by Nānak. He says, 'the entire world is suffering' *Nanak, Dukhiya sab* Sansār). In Sikhism, however, the end of misery and suffering has been made dependent on the Name (Nam) and Grace of God, and not on cessation of worldly passion as is the case in Buddhism.

The word '*Nirvānā (Pāli : Nibbāna*) was first of all used by the Enlightened One and denotes highest bliss or a state of everlasting peace. The attainment of *Nirvānā* means extinction of lust, hate, and delusion which results in cessation of misery and suffering. In Sikhism also, the word is used with almost the same import and meaning. Here it means realisation of God which, in other words means cessation of worldly misery and suffering. Further, it is significant that Guru Tegh Bahadur, the ninth Guru, while giving the definition of *Nirvānā* refers to the Buddha and says that it is the hardest thing to achieve :

"And that seeks the blissful *Nirvāna,* Nānak, That seeking is the hardest of all games :

Only the rare Enlightened Ones master it."[5]

There are four principal centres of pilgrimage for the Buddhists. These are : Lumbini, the birth place of the Buddha; Bodh Gaya : the seat of His Enlightenment; Sarnath : the place where He delivered His First Sermon, and Kushinara, the site of His *Mahā-parinirvāna.* Every year, lakhs of devout Buddhists from all over the world visit these four sacred shrines. The Sikhs too have four important pilgrim centres which are also known as four *Takhats* or Thrones of Panthic Authority[6]. These are ; Amritsar where Guru Arjun Dev compilted the Ādi-Granth; Patna (Bihar), the birth-place of Guru Gobind Singh; Anandpur, where the *Khalsa* was born; and Nander (Andhra), where Guru Gobind Singh breathed his last. As is evident, the selection of the four Sikh shrines almost follows the Buddhist pattern.

In the hey day of Buddhism, the *Vihāras* were the places where not only monks but lay people also could get food and shelter, whenever in need. The system of *'Guru Ka Langar'* food for every body in vogue in the *Gurudwaras* seems to have been adopeted by the Sikh Gurus by taking cue from the Buddhist tradition prevalent amongst some *Yogis*. Further, the Gurus seem to have constructed the Golden Temple, Amritsar with four gates on the pattern of the Buddhist *Vihāras*. Prior to the rise of Buddhism, the temples had only one gate. The Buddhists introduced the practice of four gates with a view to emphasize equality i.e. the *Vihāras* were open to all.

The religion of the Buddha is associated with Sikhism in another way also. One of the famous Sikh shrines is *Panjā Sāhib*, near Hasan Abdal in Cambellpur Distt., Pakistan. At the time of *Gurū* Nanak, it was known as the spring of Baba Wali. When Nānak visited that place, it is said, Wali Shah hurled a large rock at him. The Guru turned it aside with his hand. The marks of the five fingers of Nānak on the rock gave it the name of *Panjā Sāhib*,. The spring of Baba Wali at *Panjā Sāhib*, has since been identified as the tank of Nagaraja Elapatra who was a *Bhikkhū* at the time of Kashyapa Buddha. Hiuen Tsang, who visited this place in the 7th century, that is, about 800 years before *Gurū* Nanak and about 400 years before the advent of Islam in the Punjab has given interesting account of this tank. He says :

"North-west of the capital about 70 li is the tank of the Nagaraja Elapatra (1-10-po-t0 10); it is about 100 paces round, the waters are pure and sweet; lotus fllowers of various colours, which reflect different tints in their common beauty (garnish the surface); this Nāga was a *Bhikshū* who anciently, in the time of Kashypa Buddha, destroyed an Elapatra tree. Hence, at the present time, when the people of that country ask for rain or fine weather, they must go with the Śramanas to the side of the tank, and then cracking their fingers (or, in a moment), after praying for the desired object, they obtain it.[7]

The Buddhist heritage has passad on to the Sikhs in another form also. The Sikhs consider the tank in the Golden Temple, Amritsar as the most sacred. This tank was a small lake when *Gurū* Ram Das, the fourth Guru, per chance discovered it. He acclaimed it Amritsar, the tank of nectar. This tank is said to be Buddhistic in origin. It has since been identified as the famous lake of Padmasambhavea. St. Padamasambhava hailed from the Swat Valley and was a powerful apostle of *Tantrism.* He flourished in the eighth century and did a lot to propagate Buddhism in Tibet where he went in 747 A.D. The Tibetans consider him as their Guru and regard him next only to the Buddha. The name Padmasambhava means the Lotus born. According to a Tibetan Tradition[8] Padmasambhava was found by the King Indra-bodhi or Indrabhuti of Udyana or Urgyan on the petals of a lotus flower in this lake.

In olden days the pilgrims from Tibet used to visit this lake while on pilgrimage to other Buddhist shrines in the Punjab. In this connection we reproduce below what the famous Italian scholar, G. Tucci, has said about the itinerary of the Tibetan pilgrims who came to India in the 13th century.

"At the time of Stag Ts' an rasa pa there was a regular intercourse between Jalandhra and Tibet as there is even now. There is hardly any doubt that this was chiefly due to the travels of Tibetan pilgrims of the r Dsogs C'en and specially bka rgyad pa sects who used to visit the sacred places of Buddhist tradition. After r God Ts' an pa, their number must have considerably increased; to-day there is a regular intercourse along the routes and the tracks of Westrn Tibet.

From there, they descend to the holy *tirhas* of the Buddhist tradition, to Amritsar where the tank of the Golden Temple is believed to be the lake of Padmasambhava, to Bodh Gaya, to Sarnath."[9]

As is evident from the foregoing, there are not only a number of similarities between Buddhism and Sikhism but the Buddhist heritage has also passed on to Sikhism in more than one form.

References and Notes

1. *Selections of the Sacred Writings of the Sikhs*-a Unesco publication-1960, p. 43-26th hymn of the japji by Guru Nanak.
2. *Ibid.*, p. 49. 35th hymn of the *Japji*.
3. Dr. Sher Singh, *Phiosophy of Sikhism*, 1944, p. 106.
4. *Ibid.*, p. 106.
5. *Selections of the Sacred Writings of the Sikhs.* p. 206, Rag Gauri (p. 209).
6. This as well as other facts about Sikhism are based on *'Sikhism, Its Ideals and its Institutions*-by Teja Singh, 1951 edition.
7. Beal, *Travels of Hiuen Tsang*, Volume II, p. 180.
8. Waddel, *Buddhism of Tibet*, 1959, p. 380.
9. G. Tucci, *Travels of the Tibetan Pilgrims in the Swat Valley, 1940.* p. 14.

Appendix I

Chronology of Buddhism in the Punjab

B. C. 525-490 Lord Buddha visited Punjab some time during this period.

321 Chandragupta founded the Maurya dynasty.

298 Chandragupta died and his son Bindusara succeeded him.

273 *Aāoka* began to rule.

263 Aśoka embraced Buddhism. During his reign Buddhism became the State religion of India including Punjab.

232 Aśoka died.

184 Brihadratha, the last Maurya king, was assassinated by his commander-in-chief, Pushyamitra. Pushyamitra is said to have come upto Sialkot and persecuted the Buddhists on a large scale.

160 Menander (Milinda) began to rule over Punjab with Sialkot as his capital. He was converted to Buddhism by *Nāgasena.* He issued some coins with the Buddhist Wheel *(Dharmachakra)*.

100 About this time the rule of Milinda's successors came to an end.

80 Maues, the Saka leader, became the ruler of Punjab. He was the first ruler in India who issued coins with a Buddha figure.

58. Maues died.

A.C. 25 The Kushanas, who were Buddhists, started ruling over the Punjab.

78 Kanishka, the most important Kushana King, began to rule.

100 Abut this time was held at Jalandhar the fourth Buddhist Council under the Presidentship of Vasumitra.

200 The Kushana rule came to an end.

320 Chandragupta, chief of a small principality of Bihar founded the Gupta dynasty.

330 Samudragupta succeeded his father. He expanded his kingdom to cover most of India including Punjab.

Circa 400 Vasubandhu and his elder brother *Asaṅga* wrote many remarkable works on Buddhism.

401 Fa-hian visited Punjab.

415 Chandragupta II died. He was succeeded by Kumaragupta (415-455) and Sakandagupta (455-480).

480 Sakandagupta was succeeded by Buddhagupta who in turn was succeeded by Baladitya in 500 A.D. Both these Gupta kings were Buddhists.

520 Nara Vardhana reigned about this time in Thansear. He was succeeded by his son Rajya Vardhana I and grandson Aditya Vardhana.

580 Prabhakara-Vardhana, succeeded his father Aditya Vardhana. He fought valiantly against the Huns. The Huns mercilessly destroyed the Buddhist Shrines at Taxila.

606 Harsha Vardhana, the last Buddhist Emperor of India, began to rule.

630-644 Hiuen-Tsang in India. According to him, there were as many as 100 *Vihāras* and more then 5000 Buddhist monks in the Punjab.

647 Harsha died. Buddhism began to decline.

1250 Asokaballa or Asokachalla of Sapadalaksha (Siwalaks) in the Punjab visited Bodh Gaya in Bihar and donated large sums for carrying out repairs to the Great Maha Bodhi Temple. Till then, Buddhism was lingering on in the Punjab in one from or the other. Thereafter, it completely disappeared from the plains but continued to be a living faith in the high Himalayas.

1899 Anagarika Dharmapala, founder of the *Mahā* Bodhi Society of India, visited Punjab and gave lectures on Buddhism at many places. With this, began the movement of revival of Buddhism in the Punjab.

1928 Bhadant Anand Kauśalyāyān, the first Punjab Buddhist monk of modern times, was ordained as a *Bhikkhū*.

1956 Following Dr. B.R. Ambedkar's conversion to Buddhism, some of his followers in the Punjab also embraced Buddhism and the revival movement entered into a new phase in the Punjab as every where else in India.

Appendix II

Buddhism Survives in Pakistan

Muzaffar Hussain

Immediately after Indian Independence, China swallowed Tibet; Government of India failed to protest. As a result the people of Tibet were displeased. with India. No doubt that the Dalai Lama found refuge in India but the Tibetan masses continued to be the victims of Communist China's atrocities. Following the aggression of 1962, China became an ally of Pakistan. Although the Communist Government of China shunned religion, Government of Pakistan lost no opportunity to humour the Buddhists residing in Pakistan. In 1981, just as Pakistan treated Sikhs as different from Hindus, much before that, that is, in 1961, they had already begun to regard Buddhists as different from Hindus. They tried to mislead the Buddhists, impressing upon them that they had nothing in common with India. Your culture, your language, your religion–these are all different from the Hindus'. Insofar as Buddhism does not subscribe to imageworship you are nearer to Islam. To date, Islam has never come in conflict with Buddhism. There has been no warfare between Buddhists and Muslims. Therefore, all that belongs to Buddhists is safe and secure in Pakisatan. But shortly afterwards, Government of Pakistan disproved its own statement by permitting the sculpting and installation of a massive idol of Lord Buddha.

Buddhism is a legacy of India. However, after the Sino-Indian conflict Pakistan adopted a peculiar attitude towards the religion of the Buddha and his followers, calculated to prove that India had nothing to do with either. Since the attack by

China, India too has not yet recovered from this complex. India has failed to play a substantial role in Buddhsit-majority countries. In contrast, Pakistan's diplomacy has been strikingly successful in these countries. The Beijing-Rawalpindi highway which skirts the Himalyan ranges from its northern side has adversely affected India's political and economic interests. Pakistan continues to come closer to the Buddhist countries. On September 17, 1995 the University of Karachi awarded a doctorate (Ph.D) to one Salma for her research on Harshavardhan, an emperor of the Buddhist era; the then Governor of Sind as well as the Chief Minister of the province especially attended the convocation.

On the way to the Qaid-e-Azam University a diversion leading to Diplomatic Enclosure II cuts deep inside a forest, at the end of which one finds oneself facing a grand Pagoda. The Pagoda stands on a massive structure and is known as Buddhist Cultural Centre. Half the expenditure on its making was borne by the Government of Pakistan. The land was allotted free of cost. The other half was contributed by Nepal, Sri Lanka, China, Thailand and India The Centre was inaugurated on July 3, 1992 by the then President of Sri Lanka, the late Premadasa.

Speaking at the inaugural function, Pakistan's Secretary for Cultural Affairs observed that Buddhist culture was not at all alien for Pakistan, particularly for the areas around Islamabad which in historical times was known by the name of Potuhar that was a major centre of Buddhism centuries ago. Again, it was here that the world-famous Takshashila university flourished. From an elevation one can still see the ruins of the ancient seat of learning. The world's first exponent of political science Arya Chanakya (Kautilya) hailed from this place. He was educated in Takshashila where he later also taught political science. It was here that he groomed young Chandragupta, said the Secretary.

The souvenir published on this occasion carries an article which informs that Asoka the Great, a follower of the Buddhist faith, had Takshashila as his capital. As late as the third century B.C. this entire area was a major centre of Buddhist culture. The Buddha idols of these times bear a distinct influence of Persian and Iranian art. The Gandhara art was discovered here. Buddhist art and culture dominated the area from Takshashila to the Frontier Province. The article also claims that Lord Buddha had once set foot on the very ground where the function was held. It was the most important centre for Lord Buddha's meditation. The centre has a photograph of the massive bunyan tree in Islamabad which is being zealously guarded by the Department of Archaeology since a large number of historians are of the opinion that it was here that Prince Gautama attained enlightenment. It is difficult to decide whether this story being spread is actually based on some historical document or only a design to confound the scholars about the celebrated Bodhi-Vriksha (Tree of Enlightenment) in Gaya. The function created an impression as though Lord Buddha was in no way connected with Bihar.

The Centre holds a grand pooja of Lord Buddha on a large scale on every full-moon night. Buddha Purnima is a public holiday in Pakistan. The building also houses a large library which has in its proud possession about 25,000 works relating to Lord Buddha and the Buddhist culture. There is a massive golden idol of Lord Buddha installed in the temple, which was brought over from Sri Lanka. Lord Buddha's sermon at Sarnath has been graphically represented in a panel. Another picture depicts Lord Buddha in Varanasi along with the five bhikkhus. The temple also has a model of the famous Golden Pagoda of Yangoon. A hall on the left holds an exhibition of the frescoes from Ajanta. But the picture that draws everybody's attention is the one that portrays the grandeur of Takshashila university.

The pujari of this Buddha temple has an unusually long name, Palecund waham Parghar Samma Ratna, but for convenience people refer to him as Ratna. He is a native of Sri Lanka but has been working here as a temple employee. When he was asked, why the place was not called a Buddha temple but a cultural centre, he explained that since the expression temple (mandir) is anathema to Islamic countries, we got the permission to build this structure on condition that it would not be named Buddha mandir but Buddhist Cultural Centre. Ratna also said that the ambassadors of Buddhist countries along with their families visit the mandir and offer pooja on holidays. According to him the daily attendance at the mandir is about a hundred, but on a fullmoon night as many as 300 devotees congregate at the mandir and hold a night-long pooja session The five tenets of Lord Buddha are inscribed along the route in Urdu and English.

The Buddha temple also organises an annual fair on the occasion of Baisakhi. It is believed that Lord Buddha was born and also attained nirvana on the full-moon day of Vaishakha month. When an information assistant at the Centre was asked whether the library had any works of Dr. B.R.Ambedkar, he replied in the negative. Dr. Ambedkar has been a true follower of Lord Buddha, but since he was a bitter critic of Pakistan, we could not accommodate his works here, explained the official. The works of Rahul Sankrityayan and Bhadant Anand Kausalyayan are of course to be found here.

Courtesy : ORGANISER, VOL. XLVIII, No. 27, February 2, 1997, New Delhi, p. 15.

Select Bibliography

A.K.Narain –*The Indo-Greeks,* Oxford, 1957.

Albert Grundwedel –*Buddhist Art in India,* Revised and enlarged by Jas Burgess, London, 1901, Reprint Bharitya Publishing House, Varanasi, 1974.

Alexandar Cunningham –Ancient Geography of India, edited by S. N Majumdar, Calcutta, 1884, Reprint Indological Book House, Varanasi, 1963.

–*The Stupa of Bharhut. The Great Buddhist Monument,* London, 1879, Reprint

Indological Book House, Varanasi, 1962.

–*Maha Bodhi or The Great Buddhist Temple at Buddha Gaya,* London, 1892, Reprint, Indological Book House, Varanasi, 1965.

–*Report of a Tour in the Punjab,* 1879, Volume XIV, Archaeological Survey of India, New Delhi.

Bana –*Harshacarita,* translated by E.B. Cowell and F. W. Thomas, London, 1897. Reprint Motilal Bhanarsidas, Delhi 1961.

B.C.Law –Geography of Early Buddhism, London, 1932.

B.M.Barua –*Aśoka* and His Inscriptions, Calcutta, 1948, Reprint, New Age Publishers Private Limited, Calcutta, 1967.

D.C. Sircar –*Inscriptions of Asoka,* Publications Division, Ministry of Information and Broadcasting, Government of India, Delhi, 1956.

George Roerich –*Biography of Dharmaswamin a Tibetan Monk,* K.P Jayaswal Research Institute, Patna, 1959.

G.P.Malalsekera –*Distionary of Pāli Proper* Names, London, 1960.

G.Tucci –*Travels of the Tibeten Pilgrims in the Swat Valley,* Greater India Society, Calcutta, 1940.

H.A.Giles –*The Travels of Fa-hian or Record of the Buddhistic Kingdoms,* Cambridge, 1923, Reprint, Indological Book House Delhi, Varanasi, 1972.

Harcharan Singh Sobti –*Studies in Buddhism and Sikhism,* Eastern Book Linker, Delhi 1986.

John Marshal, Sir –*A Guide to Taxila*, Cambridge, 1951.

–*The Indus Civilization*, Cambridge, 1953.

J. Przyluski –*Ancient Peoples of the Punjab*, Audumbaras and the Salves, Indian Studies Past and Present, Translated by Chitrabhanu Sen, Calcutta, 1960.

K.N.Nilakanta Shastri –*Age of the Nandas and Mauryas*, Motilal Banarsidas, 2nd edition, Delhi, 1967.

L.A.Wadell –*Buddhism of Tibet or Lamaism*, London, 1895.

Reprint, Heritage Publishers, new Delhi-1974.

Mortimer Wheeler –Early India and Pakistan, Taraporewala, Bombay, 1959

Nandolal Dey –*The Grographical Dictionary of Ancient and Mediaval India*, Luzac, London, 1927

Punjab District Gazetteers –*Jullundur District*, 1908, Volume, XIV.

–*Kangra District*, 1904, Volume XA, Part A.

–*Karnal District*, 1918, Volume VIA.

–*Hissar District*, 1915, Volume IIA, Part A.

–*Ludhiana District*, 1904, Volume XV A.

–*Mandi State*, 1920.

–The Imperial Gazetter of India, 1908, Volume XIV.

P.V.Bapat (Ed.) –2,500 *Years of Buddhism*, Publications Division, Ministry of Information & Broadcasting, Government of India, Delhi, 1956.

Radhakumud Mookerji –*Chinese Accounts of India-Travels of Hiuen Tsiang*, Delhi, 1957.

–*Life of Hiuen Tsiang by Hui Li*, London, 1914.

Rama Shankar Tripathi –*History of Ancient India*, Motilal Banarasidas, Delhi, 1942.

Samuel Beal –*Buddhist Records of the Western world*-translated from the Chinese of Hiuen Tsiang, Motilal Banarasidas, Delhi, 1981 Edition.

Sher Singh –*Philosophy of Sikhism*, Sikh University Press, Lahore, 1944

S.M. Latif –*History of the Punjab*, 1891, Reprint, Eurasia Publishing House, Calcutta, 1964.

S.N.Sen –*India through Chinese Eyes*, University of Madras, Madras, 1956.

S.P. Gupta –*Kushana Sculptures from Sanghol*, National Museum, New Delhi, 1986.

S.Radhakrishnan –*Indian Philosophy*, Volume, I. Macmillian, London, 1958 Edition.

Stuart Piggot –*Pre-historic India,* London, 1950.

Teja Singh –*Sikhism : Its Ideals and its Institutions,* Longmans, New Delhi, 1951.

Thomas Watters –*On Yuan Chwang's Travels in India,* London, 1904-05, Reprint, Delhi, 1961.

Trilochan Singh el. at –*Selections from the Sacred Writings of the Sikhs,* a UNESCO Publication, George Allen & Unwin, London, 1960.

V.A.Smith –*Early History of India,* Oxford, 1924.

W.W.Tarn –*The Greeks in Bactaria and India,* Cambridge, 1951.

A Pakistani Buddhist Buddhism in Pakistan, Pakistan Publications, Karachi, 1954.

Index